TRANSITION IN GREEN

By

Linda Lanterman

This novel is a work of fiction. All characters are fictitious with the exception of Governor Linda Lingle, included to frame the narrative. The circumstances and actions of the governor's scene are imaginary.

ISBN: 1-4107-8871-7 (e-book)
ISBN: 1-4107-8872-5 (Paperback)

Library of Congress Control Number: 2003095907

This book is printed on acid free paper.

Printed in the United States of America
Bloomington, IN

Front cover photo by Leo's Photography

1stBooks – rev. 08/14/03

For Bentley, Davis, Alexa and Luke

Acknowledgements

For rescue at sea, the courageous and capable Paul Goubeia with EcoTours, and Captain Zodiak at Honokohau Harbor, *Hapa Lapa's* captain Alan Borowski, and dear friends Diane and Konstantin Titov.

For research assistance, writer Jean Cleaves showed me her Chinese jade constellation ring and permitted me to weave it into my story. My thanks also to Amy Hill, Larry and Loxie Hite, the Honorable Dennis Coupe, Joanne and the staff at the Hawaii Department of Natural Resources, Division of Recreation and Boating, Honokohau Harbor, to Patti Coupe and Brandon and Natalie Coupe, Kim and Jim Jennings, Joel Nelson, Charter Captain Fran O'Brien, the National Geographic Society, Norm and Natalie Pond and Marty and Suzy McNally.

To my writers' group, Sierra Writers and especially to RD Larson, Carmen Reggio, and Jeri Marie Bartow, Ann Elliott, Mary Rosseau, and Livvy Coupe.

To Dennis Mock-Chew, the crew at the Harbor House, especially Tami, Erin, Michelle, Dawn and Ester and their boss, Chihomi.

To fishing buddies, Nick Martin and Danette Mettler, Art and Kathy Ryan and Jim and Metta Keenan. In memory of Margaret and to my husband, Doug, and to our family, fair winds and calm seas.

Chapter 1

At airports or bus terminals Rick Horner always bought something he knew he wouldn't read, *The Wall Street Journal*, if he could get it. Rick stood in the check-in line for Northwest Flight 78 to Seattle. He studied the tall, skinny blonde ahead of him and feigned boredom.

When Amy Roth pulled her driver's license from her purse, her lipstick rolled off the counter. She leaned over to retrieve her lipstick and dropped her purse. A small shopping bag from *Le Bon Marché* tore and spilled a gift-wrapped box on the floor. Rick glanced up a second with hard eyes and a twitch of his jaw. He resumed looking at the same page of his folded *Newsweek*, his prop du jour. Nine other Spokane passengers joined the flight for the Seattle leg, the usual, two couples, two college kids, an older black dude, and Blondie. No cops.

"Hi, beautiful." Rick fixed his attention on the pert, brunette ticket agent. She blushed and giggled. She brushed his hand when she took his driver's license. She made mistakes as she keyed in his ticket

1

information and had to redo it twice. Rick expected it. He focused intently on her, forced warmth into his smile and asked for a seat next to the blonde who preceded him. "She seems nervous. I can show her the ropes, keep her calm. I fly all the time."

The ticket agent became an instant co-conspirator and said, "That's a middle seat, Mr. Horner. She has the window. I could put you on the aisle, one row back. Flight originates in Chicago so we don't have much flexibility."

"Piece of cake. The middle seat is fine. She needs someone to look after her."

He chuckled to himself. This is going to be easy. In the men's room he checked his teeth, his hair, his best smile. He'd done this so many times. Piece of cake.

Amy sat alone. It was June, a lovely time of year in the Spokane Valley. If she wondered about leaving her hometown, she knew she had no reason to stay. A drop of sweat ran down her backbone. Her high heels pinched. She glanced around and realized she was overdressed compared to the other passengers waiting in the terminal. She wore a strand of faux pearls over a matching light green sweater set and a black gabardine skirt. She pulled her itinerary from her ticket jacket, reread it and ran her fingers over SFO as if she didn't really believe she was on her way to San Francisco. She put the paper away and tugged at her skirt as it crept above her knee. She clasped her hands in her lap and tried not to fidget. The molded, black plastic seats proved hard and uncomfortable. A few people browsed the shop or the food concession area. Fewer sat.

Passenger Argus Pritchett yawned and ran his hand back and forth over his forehead. He tried to choke down one more swallow of bitter, lukewarm coffee. The travel desk at the Los Angeles Sanitation Department had picked up the cheapest fare for his conference in Chicago, with a stop in Helena on his return. His recycling presentation to members of the governor's staff in Montana generated some enthusiasm, but not as much as he'd hoped. Engine trouble forced him to layover in Spokane and to take Flight 78 today. He slept badly in the motel room the airline provided. He had not previously visited the city and was unlikely to return.

From habit he surveyed the terminal and picked up the familiar drama unfolding. Pritchett's eyes narrowed, the right side of his face grimaced. He sighed and noted every detail about the handsome man and his mark.

Caucasian male, 5 feet 10 inches, 190, 38 to 40 years old, hazel eyes, dark, wavy hair, possibly dyed. Roman nose, strong jaw. Ruby ring with small diamond-like stones on left hand, custom shirt, but off-the-rack pants and sports coat. No tie. Expensive, black leather carry-on. Short, stubby fingers. Chews his left thumbnail.

White female, 5 feet 8 inches or 5 feet 9, 122, 17 to 22, blue eyes, blond hair, long and straight with bangs. Eyes droop slightly at outside edges, sharp, high-bridged nose, thin, narrow face, a slightly crooked front tooth, small mouth, full lips. Attractive.

Probably has ten bucks hidden in her shoe. Nervous. *Bet you're a hometown kid on your big venture into the world. And that scum has a bead on you before you get on the plane.*

Argus shook his head. *Once a vice cop, always a vice cop. Give it a rest, old man.*

The loudspeaker announced boarding for Flight 78. Rick Horner hurried to the gate, then stopped for Amy to precede him. Aboard, he helped her stow her carry-on and introduced himself as they climbed over a sleepy, elderly man with two hearing aids.

Amy couldn't look directly at Rick for more than a moment. Her gaze darted in all directions. Airborne, she talked too fast. She dribbled her 7UP and pulled so hard on her bag of peanuts, they scattered.

There was no movie. The smell of stale air and old upholstery permeated the plane. Horner took Amy's hand when she reached up to turn on the air above her seat. He held it a second too long.

"Let me get that for you."

She pulled away and tucked her hand under her elbow next to the window. Horner kept the conversation going all the way to Seattle.

On the aisle, one row back, Argus Pritchett listened to Amy's nervous giggles and the running chatter. She had the habit of covering her mouth and nose with one hand when she laughed. He learned the young woman's name and her life history. She'd decided to quit smoking. It made her allergies worse. She wore a nicotine patch on her arm, under her blouse. She had flown twice, the short hop over to Missoula, then back, with her parents. She wanted to attend the University of Montana, but with the out-of-state fees, she'd opted instead for Washington State University at Pullman.

She liked college and earned good grades. Her life reversed direction when her parents died. Amy, with her nervous chatter, stumbled into a place she had not meant to go. She stopped. She drew several deep breaths. Her eyes filled.

Rick offered his handkerchief. "Tell me how it happened."

"Thanks." Amy unfolded his handkerchief as she talked. "They hit black ice, skidded off a bridge approach into the Spokane River and drowned."

"Where were you?"

"On my way home from college, Christmas vacation my sophomore year." Amy paused to gulp for air and dab her eyes. "I don't know they were dead. The message was to come to the hospital. No one was very helpful. Or, maybe they wanted to spare my feelings, but…"

"You suspected the worst."

"I guess so. I remember a tiled hallway and a *Morgue* sign over double doors. I'd sunk down the wall to the floor. An orderly found me with my knees drawn up, sobbing. He lifted me to a chair. I was slimy with snot and tears."

Rick said nothing. He nodded his head and waited.

"Sorry. Didn't mean to get all weepy. Anyhow, I took charge of my life."

Amy blew her nose in Rick's handkerchief. "So, in the middle of my sophomore year I left college. Had to really. Low on funds.

"I put myself through business school and took a job as a paralegal with Wales, Stanley and Bowstrom, downtown. They were good to me. Worked there two years. Pay was pretty good. I was the only young person in the office, though. After a while decided I needed a change, but nothing else in Spokane paid as well." Amy smiled to herself.

Horner noticed. "What?"

"Oh, nothing. A comment the mail clerk made."

"Tell me. Was it about your boss?"

"Yeah. All the attorneys in the office. It's rude."

"Tell me."

"He said they were all so old they must fart dust."

Amy reddened. Horner laughed, and one row back, Pritchett grimaced and raised his eyes toward heaven.

Rick asked Amy more about herself, and she told him. She lived in a declining suburb called Dishman, east of the city. When Horner asked her what she meant by 'declining,' she held her hand at a steep incline and said, "Sliding downhill. The old theater on the main street became a strip joint. The Swedish Bakery closed. The big Sperry Flower Mill in the area closed. Jobs dried up. The Navy left years ago. The Air Force cut way back."

"You have no family at all?"

"Only Auntie Thora in California. In Bakersfield. She's kinda old. Mom used to worry about her, but she seems to be fine."

"So you're going to Bakersfield, then."

"No. San Francisco. Much more exciting than Bakersfield. I think my chances for a good job are better in San Francisco."

"You've never been to California, right?"

It took all Argus' self-control not to stand up, tap Amy on the shoulder and tell her to clam-up. *It's a trap, peach blossom.* Argus' elbow rested on the armrest, his head balanced between his fingertips and his thumb.

The creep moved fast and kept talking. "We consider ourselves an extension of the Seattle Convention and Visitors' Bureau. Like an arm of the Chamber of Commerce," said Horner. He produced his business card for Amy and read it to her. "Wildside Escort and Catering. Ace Wildside, Proprietor. Rick Horner, Associate. Keep it, babe. If you're looking for work, we could put you on right away."

Finally, Amy grew quiet. Argus pinched his nose. *Too late. He has all he needs, sweetheart. Watch your purse when you get off the plane. His hook's barbed and baited.*

Horner went forward when the captain announced the approach to Seattle. Argus rose, stepped over the old man dozing on the aisle and swung into Horner's seat. He leaned close to the startled young woman and talked fast.

"The man's bad news, little sister. Argus Pritchett, twenty years with LAPD. Fifteen in vice. Retired. Currently with the Sanitation Department." He extended his hand. Amy didn't take it.

"Traded one kind of garbage for another. Always been interested in recycling. Course, with

7

people it's better to keep 'em out of the bin in the first place. Amy Roth, your friend is trouble."

Amy squared her shoulders and clutched at her throat. "So, you save people?" Her head gave a stiff jerk.

"Only those who want saving. Can't help someone who chooses to ignore a warning."

"You save hayseeds who go to the big, bad city?" Color rose in her cheeks. "I can take care of myself. I know what an escort service is."

"Well now, that's good."

"We talked, that's all. Conversation."

"Hang on to your purse." Pritchett nodded up the aisle and flicked his thumb in Horner's direction. "You lose your money, your driver's license, your ID, he's got you."

"I don't know many black— I mean African-Americans." Amy gave him a weak smile and looked away.

Argus's eyes grew wider then softened. "We're just like everyone else. We share the same cultural history. We built this country, fought its wars. We share the same hopes and dreams, as all y'all."

"I apologize. I didn't mean to be rude. You're probably a nice man." She twisted her fingers. Her eyes darted back and forth.

"You get stranded in San Francisco, here's a name and number." Argus scribbled on a small notepad and tore off the sheet for Amy.

"Yeah, right. Who's this? How do I know you're not the same?"

"My sister. She's a nurse at SF General Hospital. Check it out. Oh-oh. Here comes lover boy."

Amy tucked the scrap of paper into the cuff of her sleeve.

"You're in my seat, Bub." Rick said. His voice snarled through clenched teeth.

"Excuse me." Argus rose and stepped into the aisle. His hair was shot with gray. He stood taller than Horner.

Rick hesitated, seemed unsure what to do. He hadn't noticed this guy's confident demeanor in Spokane. The men studied each other a long moment. Argus waited, relaxed, too relaxed. The light in his eyes almost begged Rick to try something. Rick Horner drew a deep breath and moved aside.

Inside the Seattle terminal, Amy headed for her new gate and her connection to San Francisco. She wore the strap of her purse across her body. She had white-knuckle grips on her purse and her carry-on. Rick tagged along, told her to keep his card, call him any time. He'd send her a plane ticket. She would love Seattle, a beautiful city.

Rick kept it short. He turned and watched Argus Pritchett watch him. He'd been wrong. There was a cop on the flight. The black guy was a cop.

Linda Lanterman

Chapter 2

In San Francisco, Amy's inexpensive hotel turned out to be south of Market Street, outside the redevelopment perimeter. In spite of her homespun looks and conservative clothes, the night clerks at first took Amy for a working girl. They supposed any female under forty was in the sex trade. When they realized she wasn't, they smirked and suggested she consider it.

"I'm a paralegal," she said and kept her door double locked.

She didn't think California could be so cold in the summer. Nor did she find the thick fog romantic. It rolled in from the sea, through the Golden Gate and washed over the hills most afternoons. Whenever the Central Valley temperatures climbed into the nineties and beyond, the heat pulled a protective marine layer over the coast. Fog turned the city gray and ruined her hairstyle. She phoned the number Argus Pritchett gave her. He'd told the truth. Someone at San Francisco General Hospital answered. The woman she asked for came to the phone, but Amy hung up.

Over and over, she congratulated herself for packing her walking shoes. She carried her dress shoes, with two-inch heels, in her black canvas bag with her resume, recommendations and transcripts. It was quick and easy to change shoes when she entered an office. Many women did the same. No one paid any attention.

On a sunny morning when Amy had no appointments she took a Gray Line Tour of the city. She was glad she did. It was a splurge, but the dramatic beauty of the city called her. She marveled at canyons of skyscrapers, buildings of all shapes and eras, the colorful Victorian homes with their common walls, and the long narrow snapshots of the Bay, the bridges, and parks which she glimpsed from the top of streets that fell away to lower levels. She saw streets with stairs for sidewalks, and flowers growing in postage stamp plots.

She learned that the San Francisco's population is more than a third Asian, and the Asian Art Museum had recently moved into the old main library building on one side of Civic Center Plaza. The $160.5 million museum project was part of the city's ten-year revitalization of the whole Civic Center. She visited Grace Cathedral, Nob Hill and the Palace of the Legion of Honor. She missed the zoo, Treasure Island and had only a quick glance at the Opera House, but he felt she understood the city better after the tour. She was not as worried about getting lost.

The next day in a tiny deli on Pine Street, Amy studied the Classified Ads in the *Chronicle*. A voice broke through her concentration.

"Split my sandwich with you if I can sit down?" A woman about her age looked at Amy with a bright, shiny face and the unnatural stare of a person with new contacts.

"Oh sure. You don't have to give me half your sandwich. Sit."

"I only eat half, anyway. Like turkey?"

"Well, sure. Thanks. I'll pay half."

"That's okay. Call it my good deed for the day. New in town? What kind of job you looking for?"

"Paralegal. I have experience and references."

"I work for a florist out in Westlake. I have two-room apartment in a basement near the Farmers' Market. Where you staying?"

"Fleabag hotel south of Market. Little scary." Amy sneezed. Another high squeak of sneeze escaped while she dug in her purse for a tissue.

"Oh, oh. You're allergic to cats, aren't you?"

"What?"

"Cats. I have four of them. I adopted them. They were running wild." The young woman brushed vigorously at the cat hairs on her jacket. "I think you're allergic."

"Must be." Amy blew her nose.

"So much for the possibility of splitting the rent." She cocked her head. "You know, you should take your sandwich to Civic Center Plaza. Lots of law clerks and office workers eat their lunches there when the weather's nice. City Hall employs a ton of lawyers. If I were you, I'd start hanging out there over the noon hour. Know how to get there?"

"Yes. Guess it's worth a try."

13

"Thanks for sharing your table. Good luck on the job search."

"Thank you." Amy held up the remainder of her half sandwich. "Nice talking with you."

When Amy went outside the sun shone though the early afternoon clouds and seemed to promise success. It didn't turn out that way.

She couldn't schedule an interview with any of the legal firms she approached. She went up and down the walkways of Civic Center Plaza the next day. When a young woman in a group of three smiled at her, she took a deep breath and struck up a conversation with them before her courage failed her. They were about her age and friendly. One happened to have the latest posting of job openings and gave it to Amy.

"Thanks. I picked up the list the second day I was in town. It just takes so long to get an interview." Amy handed the stapled sheets back. "They only give the competency test every six to eight weeks, and they gave it three days before I arrived."

"Tough break," said one of the women chewing a bite of apple. "And, even when you pass it, there are no guarantees. Get your name on the eligible list is all."

No one mentioned money, but each one probably guessed it was a problem for Amy. Over the next two weeks depression stalked her. Homeless men slept in the alleyways on either side of her building. Returning one late afternoon, Amy noticed a homeless woman with two small children. They sat on the sidewalk leaning against the rough bricks of the building near to Amy's hotel. The woman could have been younger than Amy, but her matted hair and tearstained cheeks made her look older. Amy gave her ten dollars and didn't eat that night. After nineteen days, Amy called her aunt and bought a bus ticket to Bakersfield.

*   *   *

A large, muscular man of thirty-five or forty years sat next to Amy. With a quick glance and a nod, she took in the cowboy shirt with snaps instead of buttons, the worn jeans, heavy, lace-up boots, and the black dirt in the crease lines of his hands and under his fingernails. He wore too much aftershave. He could have come from eastern Washington.

"Howdy."

"Hi."

"How far you goin'?"

"Bakersfield."

"Oh? Me too. I'm a roughneck. Know what that is?"

"Can't say that I do."

"Work on the oil rigs. We're called roughnecks."

"And proud of it." Amy gave him a weak smile, but she didn't cut him any slack.

"Darn straight. Name's Len Tweeper. What's yours, sweetie?"

"Tweeper? Amy laughed with her hand over her nose and mouth. "You're kidding?"

"That's it. The Lord's truth. What's yours?"

"Amy." She giggled again. "Sorry. I didn't mean to laugh."

"That's it? Amy?"

"Amy Roth." She instantly wished she hadn't given him her real name. It was a mistake. Len continued to chat and ask her questions.

"I'm really tired," said Amy. She yawned and almost leaned her head against the window, but a greasy smudge on the glass stopped her. She closed her eyes.

"Put your head on my shoulder if you want. It's okay with me."

"That's all right. I'm fine."

"I insist. Lean on me." Len lifted his arm around Amy's shoulders. She grabbed his fingers hard and moved his arm back.

"I'm not going to have to complain to the driver, am I?"

"No, Ma'am." Tweeper held both hands up as if she had a gun pointed at him. He kept quiet. Amy closed her eyes and pretended to rest. After a while Tweeper dug into his knapsack and pulled out a small white canister of breath spray. He discharged it twice into his mouth and put it away. Amy turned toward the window. *Gag.* The roughneck checked out the other passengers.

At a rest stop in Fresno, Amy stepped from the air-conditioned coach into the 112-degree heat and nearly fainted. The bus driver hurried to get a cup of water for her.

"Welcome to the San Joaquin Valley," he said. Other passengers assured her that 112 degrees was unusual. The temperatures would return to milder high 80s and 90s soon. They lied.

Chapter 3

The wind-up alarm clock in Aunt Thora's spare room measured the seconds with awkward jumps. Each second hammered Amy's confidence. Auntie had greeted Amy with warmth, understanding and persistent questions about how she might find a job. Amy recounted her cash, thirty-nine dollars, twenty cents. Her bank statement showed two hundred dollars, thirty-five cents without her recent forty-two dollar, seventeen cent check to K-Mart.

Amy ran her finger down the columns of the *Bakersfield Californian* Help Wanted section a second time to review the ads she marked. Three letters of application lay on the tiny, pine desk, sealed, ready to mail. She needed full time but returned to an ad with limited hours. She liked the honesty.

In home care needed for disabled man. Some lifting, personal assistance, cleaning, cooking. Driver's license and references required, also sense of humor and ability to be pleasant with cranky, order-giving, ex-military man. Mornings or afternoons 8-1 or 1-6.

Amy turned over the flimsy little card that was her temporary license. Maybe the long hours in line at Department of Motor Vehicles were worth it. She called the number. She didn't know why. She told herself she could piece a couple of jobs together, if it came to that.

"Clifford Harness Racing. This is Martha." A woman's voice gave Amy an address in Shafter, about twenty minutes northwest of town. She should be there Monday between 1 p.m. and 2:30 with her references and résumé. "Follow the drive around the main house to the stables. Park by the paddock. Go up the center stairs over the stables to the office. We have four other people to interview, so far."

*   *   *

Julie Clifford convinced her skeptical younger brother, Regis, that they could do the screening as well as any agency. The interviews discouraged them. Regis drummed his fingers, practiced deep breathing. He tried not to express his impatience. They sniped at each other between candidates. He could see the heat in her face and could feel his own stress in his increased heartbeat and his urge to yell at her. His time was more valuable than this, so was hers.

The family's secretary, Martha, gave her staccato double knock and opened the door just enough for her head. "Just two more, Mr. Clifford. Are you ready for…" she glanced at her list, "Amy Roth?"

Regis said, "Give us a minute to review her paperwork, then send her in, Martha."

"She's overqualified," said Julie after twenty seconds. We don't need computer or research skills."

"Yeah, best list I've seen all day. Says she's worked with a wide variety of personalities, but nothing about health care, no experience for what we need."

"You're right. Tell Martha skip her and send in the last one."

Regis buzzed Martha. She stepped into his office and shut the door behind her.

"Your other candidate threw up in the waste basket and left, Mr. Clifford. Too horsy for her around here, I guess. What a mess."

"Okay, send in Roth." Regis turned to Julie. "She's here. We can give her five minutes." He sorted through the other papers in front of him. "One or two of these might work."

"You kidding, aren't you?" Julie sighed and slumped in her chair, but she straightened when she saw Amy Roth. "Hmm."

Amy wore a white long-sleeved blouse with a black grosgrain ribbon at the neck, a narrow, black skirt and a wide belt that showed off her small waist. She had a small mouth with full lips, colored apple red. One front tooth slanted while her other teeth stood at attention.

Amy's right hand patted the pale, thin hair of her pageboy as if to ensure it hadn't gone straight on her. She had a whisper of bangs that curved over her eyebrows and into serious blue eyes. She looked like she came from Bismarck, North Dakota or Salmon, Idaho, a wholesome young woman trying to look sophisticated or sexy.

19

"We don't want to waste your time, Ms Roth," Julie said. "It appears you have no experience in elder care."

"But I do. I don't put it on my résumé because I hoped to continue in the paralegal field. I cared for my grandmother before she died of Alzheimer's. During the summers when I was in high school and when Mom needed a break. Grandma and I got along much better than she and my mother. I have a knack for it."

"What if something comes up in the legal field? We need someone who is reliable. Someone we know will be here, no matter what."

Regis glanced at his sister. Julie ignored him.

Amy Roth drew a long breath. "Don't think that's going to happen. I've been looking for almost five weeks, first in San Francisco, now here. I don't know California law. Don't know anyone who could open doors for me. I'm real tired of being propositioned, and I need the job." Amy looked from Julie to Regis, then at the table. "I'd be grateful enough to give two weeks notice." Her words tumbled out on top of each other.

She raised her eyes from the applications back to Regis and to Julie. Her chin jutted. "My father worked for the US Navy Supply Depot, Eastern Washington. He wasn't in the Navy, but he acted like it. I can do this job and do it well."

Regis grinned out of one corner of his mouth. Julie ran two fingers back and forth over her lips. She didn't even turn to Regis. "You're hired," she said. "Can you do a full day? We have someone who comes in overnight."

Amy's eyebrows leaped. "Sure. That's better for me."

"Good. Let's go over to the house. We'll introduce you to Dad."

Julie and Regis glanced at each other. They didn't tell Amy their father fired his last two caregivers or that a recent stroke advanced his mental and physical deterioration.

Linda Lanterman

Chapter 4

Julie and Regis found their father coherent. Amy thought Stu Clifford must have been handsome before age ravaged him. One of the family pictures in his room confirmed this. He still had a good head of wavy, silver hair. The lid of his right eye drooped closed. The good eye flickered in confusion, then glared with blue fire. His mouth gaped. He had most of his own teeth.

"You ride?" Mr. Clifford said when introduced to Amy.

"Yes, sir. Some."

The light in her eyes and her smile captivated him. His eyebrows bounced. He grinned and smacked his lips. Spittle escaped down his chin. Amy snatched a Kleenex and patted him dry.

"Commander Clifford, do you know I dreamed of having a horse of my own, when I was little? It was so exciting to ride, even if I only went in a big circle. Mother said I cried when I had to get off the pony when we went to the fair."

Julie raised her eyebrows at Regis when Amy promoted their father from lieutenant commander,

23

USN, to full commander. Each time Amy addressed him, she called him commander or sir.

Stu Clifford raised his arthritic right index finger at his grown children and said, "Rebel. Tell, tell Neil to see to it that, that she rides Rebel."

"We will, Dad," said Regis.

"That's an order."

"Yes, Dad," said Julie.

"An order. Call Neil." Stu Clifford turned his head toward the telephone. His index finger twitched. His hand wavered in mid-air.

Julie and Regis exchanged nods and tiny smiles. Regis picked up the phone. Valley Rebel, the stable's most famous trotter died before either Julie or Regis was born.

"We'll put her on Traveler," said Neil. "The old man won't know the difference by tomorrow. Traveler's calm and slow. He could use a longer workout. And, your father likes to watch the workouts. Same thing every morning, but it's all new to him."

"It's set for tomorrow morning, Dad. Neil's taking care of it." Regis saw Amy's forced smile.

"Oh! Great," she said with a little rise in her voice. She ran her hands up and down her arms. "What time do I start?"

"Workout's at 6:30 sharp," Stu Clifford said. He clamped his hand down on the arm of his wheelchair. "Dawn."

Amy swallowed. Her mouth opened, then closed.

Julie leaned over and kissed her father. "Bye, Dad. See you in a couple of days." She turned to Amy. "Regis will fill you in on the details."

Outside, Amy said, "Mr. Clifford, I have to tell you I don't know how to ride. I never thought he'd...Well, I think most little girls dream of riding their own horse, but...Did I miss something in the job description?"

Regis laughed. "Don't worry about it. Are you willing to try? Dad forgets things. All you have to do is try. Julie has some boots and old gear in the back closet of the stable office. Should fit you. Go back up there and ask Martha for Julie's box of clothes. We'll pay you for the extra hours."

"Mr. Clifford, other than four or five pony rides at the fair, I've been on a real horse twice in my whole life. I'll try, but you might as well ask me to operate a bulldozer."

Linda Lanterman

Chapter 5

Amy never had a more coherent conversation with Stu Clifford than she did at their first meeting. Over the next few weeks and months, a series of mini-strokes kept him in and out of the hospital where, each time, doctors worked to stabilize him and return him home. The busy, late summer racing season was in full swing. Temperatures in Shafter at the stables hit 112 degrees. Outdoor activity stopped during midday. Regis and Julie appreciated Amy's willingness to help in the office when their father was hospitalized. They needed her help.

During her first couple of months with Clifford Stables, Amy tried to master riding under the supervision of the head trainer, Neil Ericson. At sunrise, the commander watched from his wheelchair, head slumped to one side. A long cloth bound him, under his arms, to the back of his wheelchair in a semi-upright position. Today, he dozed, mouth agape, awoke with fitful starts, dozed again. He wouldn't see Amy ride this morning.

She limped painfully to a bench and tried to get her boot off. Traveler had moved suddenly in his stall and nailed her foot.

"Can't ride today. He stepped on my foot," said Amy when Neil came to help.

"Don't worry about the old man. The paddock calms him," said Neil when he saw Amy watching the commander from a distance. "Something in the energy, the horses and trainers, the dust rising with the dawn, reaches him."

"The commander's getting worse," said Amy. "He manages just a word or two a day, words like *yeah* or *okay* or *ow*." Amy dropped her boot. "Sometimes he communicates by staring at things, but usually there's only confusion there, behind his eyes. He responds to touch, though. Squeezes my hand sometimes when I ask him questions."

"I notice you skip your morning ride whenever he's in the hospital," said Neil.

"Yeah, I know." Amy grinned. "I'm not much of a rider, Neil."

"You don't have to continue the lessons, gal. I can see you'll never be at ease." Neil squinted against the rising winter sun. "Sorry Traveler stepped on your foot. I'll get some ice then I'll give Martha a call and tell her you'll be late. Stay here. We need to soak your foot in ice water, cold as you can stand it. Hope no toes are broken. Can't do much for toes."

Amy bit her lip. "He didn't mean it. Not like some of the other horses."

"Nah, Traveler's a good ol' horse. Look at that." Traveler swung around nuzzled the back of Amy's shirt.

"Oh!" Amy tried to duck away, but she didn't move fast enough. "He's slobbering on me."

"Saying he's sorry. That's all."

"I know. He's very sweet." She limped out of Traveler's reach. "It's not like I'm going into a show ring or anything. Maybe I could learn on one of the ponies."

"Damn ponies bite, Amy. You should stay with Traveler."

"I'm afraid I'll fall."

"Tell you what. You come on out here every mornin' and sit with Mr. Clifford. Wipe his nose. Keep him straight in his chair, talk to him, and we'll forget the riding. How's that?"

Amy leaped and threw her arms around Neil. "Thank you!"

"Whoa. Last time I got a hug like that was when I asked Verna to marry me."

*   *   *

Amy took night classes at the community college. She wanted to work on all the undergraduate prerequisites she could. At work she'd impressed Martha from the first day when she offered to assist in the office. Martha had plenty for her to do.

She had told Amy that Julie Clifford came out to the stables about once a month to visit their father and help oversee the operation.

"Regis has the legal authorization to run the stables and to distribute paychecks, but you'll notice that he wisely includes his sister in the administration. Until Stu Clifford dies, their father owns it all."

Amy limped painfully up the stairs and found brother and sister in the office. *Oh, great. First day I'm late and they're both here.*

She need not have worried. Regis and Julie didn't seem to notice.

"We're shifting you to office management, Amy, if it's okay with you. Dad needs a full-time nurse," Julie said.

"Martha's told us how much you've helped her out. You go way beyond your job description," said Regis. "We're prepared to up your salary a bit."

"Of course, it wouldn't be as much as Martha makes," Julie said with a look at Regis.

"Amy helped me convert and update the files." Martha seemed eager to bolster Amy's case. "I have the hang of the new applications now! She went through them with me. If I have a question, she usually has the answer."

"I'd like to keep a few of my duties with the commander, if I may. He's such a nice old guy."

"Sure. Like what?"

"Oh, I could help feed him part of the time. Talk to him, even though he can't talk back."

"Probably a good idea," said Julie. "You settle him. Neil said he was screaming incoherently this morning until you arrived."

"Julie," said Regis. "You know what the doctor told us. It's going to get worse."

That was the case. In spite of a sling for lifting the commander into and out of his bed and the bath, his needs became too great. Within weeks, Julie and Regis moved him to Sunny Hills. Stu Clifford squeezed Amy's hand when she said good-bye. Amy pressed her lips together and tried to hold back tears.

*   *   *

She walked the roadways and the paddocks in the early mornings. It was either that or swimming laps. Regis had told her she could use the lap pool at the stables. Walking was easier on her hair, unless there was tule fog, the valley's thick, wet blanket of ground fog that rises in winter to blind and obscure everything. On good days, the sun burned off the fog by mid-morning. In the winter's early morning tule fog, Amy might as well have been in a pool. She called her damp, early morning walks therapy sessions. She missed the commander, and living with Aunt Thora had its ups and downs.

"Nothing deters Auntie Thora," said Amy when Martha asked what was bothering her. "Auntie Thora dragged me to her square dance group at the Odd Fellows Lodge. Between tobacco breath and those old buzzards stepping on my toes, I decided to develop back pain so bad that I can't square dance ever again. It isn't just that.

"She has tried to set me up with her banker, the director of a funeral parlor, our postman and a guy making pizza." Amy's face took on a crazed expression and she held up her hands like stiff claws. "These guys range in age from about eighteen to fifty-nine, and the postman's married!"

"Don't worry, Amy. She's trying to make you happy."

"She's trying too hard, Martha."

31

*   *   *

In February Amy heard a rumor that Regis and Julie would sell the stables when the old man died. She went to find Neil. "I don't believe it," she said.

"Me neither," said Neil. "They hired you, what? Six, eight months ago? And we just hired another trainer, Mitch Webber. You met Mitch?"

Amy nodded.

"So, I don't know about any change. We have three good trotters coming up for next season. I'm ready for retirement. Several of these guys are. It's the young people like you, Mitch and the younger grooms might get left in the lurch. He thinks you're kinda cute, by the way."

"What? Who?" Amy frowned.

"Mitch Webber, the new guy. Mentioned your long legs and nice a—ah, attitude."

"My attitude!" Amy laughed in spite of herself. Her hand cupped over her mouth and nose. It was flattering to be noticed, but it was also creepy. She went out of her way to avoid Mr. Mitch Webber. She succeeded until the night of the party, the month-end beer bust.

Amy and Martha headed from the office to Amy's car when Neil intercepted them.

"Hey. Ladies. Come on over. Join the group for a few minutes."

"Need to get Martha home. Gotta get back to Bakersfield," said Amy. Her hands fanned out as if there were nothing she could do.

"Oh, I suppose we could stop in for a few minutes, Amy. No one smokes." Martha said.

"My aunt's expecting me."

"Give her a call," Neil said.

Amy didn't bother. Aunt Thora would tell her to stay. She might meet someone. "Fluff your hair, dear. Shoulders back, boobs out." Auntie's favorite line.

Amy knew all the stable guys, a nice group on the whole. None she considered dating, but she plastered on a smile and trailed Martha to the back of the paddock where sycamores sent long shadows across picnic benches near the pond. The sun dropped behind the Coast Range across the valley. Clouds blotted out the lingering rays, and the sky turned dark. Strings of electric lights lit the picnic area.

No harm in stopping a few minutes, I guess.

Mitch Webber came forward with two beers and offered them to the women. "Nothing better after a hard day's work," he said.

"Hate beer. Any Diet Coke?" said Amy.

"Nope, just beer."

Amy knew better. She placed the orders for the food and drink. She moved around Mitch toward the ice tubs.

"Try a sip. I promise you'll like it. Nothing better to wash away the dust," Mitch said.

"I'm getting hot coffee," said Martha. "Chilly out here."

"Give mine to Neil," Amy said to Mitch. "Or, drink it yourself." She reached into the cold slushy water and fished out a Diet Coke. Regis nodded to her, and she headed to the table where he stood talking to a

33

groom everyone called Doughnut. Mitch didn't follow her.

She asked Regis about the rumor she'd heard. He laughed and put it to rest. "No, I love trotters. Julie wants out. I plan to buy her half and keep racing. It's no secret. Glad you asked. Don't want to worry any of you folks."

Amy finished her Coke and collected Martha. They said their good-byes and headed back to the car.

"Kinda dark along here, isn't it?" Martha picked her way carefully. "Don't want to step in anything."

"Yeah. Shouldn't those lights be on along here?" Amy pointed to a string of unlit light bulbs overhead. The women felt their way along the dark backside of a row of stalls. The smell of horses and hay filled their nostrils. "Lights should be on. Any idea where the switch is?"

"Don't come out here much. Slow down," said Martha. "I can't see."

Large overhead lights in the distant parking area cast fuzzy balls of light that foretold tule fog. Amy shivered in the damp night air. *Keep calm. Nothing to be afraid of. Keep calm.* She jumped sideways at a noise. *Horses. Horses in their stalls.*

She walked faster, leaving Martha behind. She wanted to run. Her right hand extended toward the stable wall, to catch herself if she tripped. She swallowed hard and called out to Martha without turning around. "Wait there. I'll get the car and come back for you."

Another noise, not a horse. Amy froze. Gravel scraped, then crunched. A footstep. She couldn't breathe.

"You're a good-looking woman, Amy. I could be interested in you." Mitch Webber's voice came from her right at the same time he grabbed her arm above the elbow and swung her into the side of the stable. Amy gasped so much air she nearly choked.

"Let go!"

"Just a kiss. I've wanted to do this for a long time." Mitch crushed her mouth as he pinned her body against the siding. Splinters jabbed her.

"Amy?" Martha's voice called out in the darkness, then louder, "Neil! Neil!"

"That you, Martha?" Neil's voice, farther away. "What the hell happened to the lights?"

Mitch pulled his head away but held Amy fast. She coughed and gagged. "Get away from me! Let go of me! Martha!"

Martha came up with Neil close behind her. "Amy?"

"Help me get away from this creep!" She pushed away as Mitch loosened his grip.

"What's the problem?" Neil's voice was close now.

"Why didn't you help me?" Amy swung around to face the shadow that was Neil. Her voice shook with brittle anger. "Why didn't you help me?"

"What's going on? I just got here, Amy."

Amy grabbed Martha's hand. She spoke to Mitch as she yanked Martha after her. Full-blown rage edged her words. "Don't you ever come near me again!"

*   *   *

Amy sped onto Highway 99 heading into Bakersfield. Martha made several attempts to get her seatbelt buckled. Amy's nose ran into her mouth and tears dripped from her chin before she realized she was crying.

Chapter 6

"So the guy stole a kiss. You're okay. Get a grip."

Martha's attitude made Amy stare at her in shock. She swerved into the slow lane.

"Take control before you have an accident, Amy! Listen to me! Hang onto your anger, but take control of it. Here's a Kleenex. Want me to drive?"

Amy used the tissue and two more. "You're right, but what a jerk!"

"Stay alert. Never, never go out with him. Don't permit yourself to be alone with him. If he comes into the office, and I'm not there, keep the door open. Better yet, leave. Go outside and talk to one of the grooms.

"You get a creepy feeling about someone, Amy, trust it. Learn to scream, really scream, at the first sign of trouble."

Amy nodded. She looked over at Martha and thought how prim and square she appeared. Martha caught the look and Amy's unspoken question.

"Experience," she said and turned away.

At that moment Amy resolved to become mentally tougher. On Monday, when Neil asked her how she was, she answered in a quiet, controlled voice. "You should have helped me."

"Amy, gal, it was dark. I've spoken to him. When I got there I saw two shadows standing together and Martha flapping her arms."

"Well, thank goodness you came along. And, in case you had any doubts, I have an extremely low opinion of Mitch."

*   *   *

Webber stayed away from the office for the next few weeks. He took pains to go the other way if he saw Amy around the stables. She noticed a yellowing bruise on the left side of his jaw.

Amy stopped her early morning walks. She talked to her aunt about other jobs. She kept it vague and skipped the Webber episode. Auntie might think it was great that someone was so interested in her.

Over dinner one evening before Amy rushed off to her class, Aunt Thora cocked her head and said, "Had my teeth cleaned today. Dr. Phister said you're getting braces."

Thora studied her niece and waited. Amy made no response. "He said you asked for the ugliest braces he had."

"A joke, Auntie. I asked for braces to straighten this." Amy tapped her front tooth. "It's always bothered me. Since braces are ugly, I made a joke of it."

"You don't need braces. You're a beautiful girl. One tooth a little slanted is nothing. No one notices. You're too sensitive, Amy, dear."

Amy had her braces by the end of the week. On the surface things continued as usual, but she updated her résumé.

*   *   *

Neil stood at Amy's desk and double-checked his purchase order for feed. "You don't take your morning walks anymore. Anything wrong?"

"Oh, no. Need some extra focus on my course work is all."

"If you want to ride, let me know. Mitch said he'd give you some lessons on his own time. I told him you didn't take to it, but he insists he can teach anyone. He asked me to mention it. Said he was sorry for the earlier misunderstanding. Said he'd like to make it up to you."

Amy didn't look up. She didn't pause. "Actually, I've talked to the woman from Button Willow who teaches at the college. Dressage. You control the horse with your knees and legs, body movements, to free the hands for weapons. It has a long history. A style of riding originally developed for battle, long before tanks and such. I can get physical education credit for it."

"Hmm. Mitch doesn't know dressage."

"Julie gave me a couple of her vanilla riding breeches and the riding gear she left here. I'm all set."

Her lie was smooth, but she realized she rambled too long. Neil scratched his head and looked at the floor. Across the room, Martha's surprised expression drew a fierce glare from Amy.

Martha recovered and said, "I told Amy, we could shorten our lunch hour so we could leave a little early on the days she has lessons."

"Oh," said Neil. He turned to leave then turned back. "Almost forgot. I better call the vet again. I talked to him early this morning. The colt he looked at last night is still down."

"What?" Both Amy and Martha spoke at once.

"Midnight Racer drank some insecticide. Afraid we're goin'a lose him."

"How awful!" Amy knew the colt. She rose to leave the office. "How could it happen? Insecticide?"

"Goddamned stupidity, if you ask me. Spraying for weeds around the paddock. Gardener leaves his refill bucket close to the fence. The colt sticks his head out and drinks. Thinks it's water. That's why I didn't get in here earlier. Afraid we're goin'a lose him. Be hell to pay."

The colt had a stall near the office. Amy sometimes stopped to rub his ears and pat him. She pounded down the steps and ran out to closest paddock. No colt. *It isn't true.* Then she saw the dark form in the second paddock. The colt was down, legs folded under him. He held his head and ears up, but his eyes were dull. Flies crawled on his nose and ventured in and out of his mouth. She could see his tongue.

"Hey, Midnight. Midnight. Sweet fella. Come on, Midnight. Sweet fella." The colt's head dipped at her words, but he didn't focus. His head stayed down. "Oh, God, don't let him die." She whispered into her hands. "Please. Please."

Neil came over and put his arm over her shoulder. "We've done everything we can. Regis is on his way. You better leave now. Go on. I told Martha you gals should take off. She's waiting for you."

It was Martha's day to drive. "Sad. Such a beautiful animal."

"I can't stand it, Martha. I can't."

"It was an accident, Amy, a terrible accident."

"It was stupid!"

The colt was gone when Amy and Martha arrived the next morning. They didn't ask about him. They knew.

Before the noon break, Amy told Regis she needed to talk with him.

"Come into my office," he said. Taller than she, Regis looked down and watched her with a mixture of concern and dread.

He knows. He knows what I'm going to say. And, he did. He explained about the colt and how sorry he was. He asked if there had been any more trouble with Mitch or any of the others. He told her how much he valued her work, but he could see it was all too late. Amy asked for a recommendation. Regis agreed and even suggested some people for her to contact in Los Angeles.

"I think I'll go back to the Bay Area. Give it a second chance. I judged it pretty harshly the first time."

Regis ran through his Rolodex. "Think my contact up there has moved. Let me check with Julie. See if she knows anyone you could contact."

"I appreciate it."

"You've done a good job, Amy. Would a pay raise make you reconsider?"

"You've been great, Mr. Clifford. I need to go."

*　　*　　*

Amy picked up two porterhouse steaks and a bottle of Chianti on her way home. She had the lettuce rinsed and the tomatoes cut into wedges when Aunt Thora, smelling of cigarette smoke, returned from her bridge group across the street.

"Oh my goodness, steak! You don't like red meat that much. It's not my birthday. What are we celebrating?"

"Gave my two weeks notice, Auntie. I feel like I could walk on the clouds. I plan to focus full-time on my classes, then head back to the Bay Area in June.

Aunt Thora smiled her sweet-sad smile, settled into a kitchen chair like a deflated balloon and said, "I knew this day would come."

After dinner, they moved to the back porch so Aunt Thora could light her Virginia Slims.

"What a beautiful twilight," said Amy. She looked from the sky to the full ashtray and economy-sized can of Raid by Aunt Thora's rocker. Trying not to be obvious, she pulled one of the white resin chairs over by the wooden railing away from the smoke.

"You've been so kind, Auntie. At least you'll be able to enjoy a cigarette in your own house without having to worry about my allergies."

"It's a nasty habit. If I could quit, I would."

They chatted long into the evening. Thora told Amy about her Bridge game. Amy told her aunt about the colt that drank the insecticide. Thora tried to console Amy.

"I understand how a thing like that would make you feel, but it was an accident."

"There were others things, too."

Aunt Thora looked up. Amy kept it light. "Little things."

Aunt Thora didn't press, but she invariably touched on Amy's lack of suitors. Amy let it pass. The few dates she'd had discouraged or frightened her. She could have done as well in Dishman. She changed the subject.

"One more riding lesson in dressage. Last one tomorrow."

"Do you like it any better than the riding you did at work?"

"No, riding and I don't mix. Beautiful animals, but I haven't conquered my fear of them. Anyway, I think it's best to leave, to start fresh. If I stay here, I'll die of Valley Fever or become ground into dust at the edge of a cotton field or under the hooves of the horses," she said.

Ants swarmed at one end of the back porch, their frantic motion silent to human hears. Thora whipped out her Raid and went after them. The smell of insecticide hung in the air.

"Let's go inside," said Amy.

*   *   *

Aunt Thora sat in a worn winged-back chair and crocheted another doily. Images flickered in silence on a muted television screen. If she stayed, Amy saw herself following a path that would turn her into her mother or her aunt.

"I owe you and the Clifford family everything, Auntie Thora. You have been so generous letting me stay here and letting me use your car. But I have to leave."

"It will be lonely without you, Amy. Kinda expected you'd leave. So many of the young people leave. I want you to take the car. I don't need it. I haven't driven since I ran through the zinnias by the driveway the day I hit the yield sign downtown. That was a couple of weeks before you came. I have my grocery carrier and my friends and the bus."

"I'd like to pay for the car as soon as I get settled in a new job."

"That's fine. You take your time, dear. Don't worry about it. The job's the thing. Finding another job."

Chapter 7

In the warm season of dragonflies, bass patrol in circles over gravel nests. Harv ran his hand over his mouth and tried to figure out where he'd gone wrong. He stared at the damselflies without really seeing them. Bass favor the damselfly, a small, blue version of the larger dragonfly. To catch them, the young fish leap and sometimes land on shore or a dock and cannot flop their way back to the water. Harv walked along the edge of the pond. He found three dead bass no longer than his thumb. Ants eat the eyes first. Harv nudged one of the tiny fish back into the water with his toe. He could not spend another year in Bakersfield.

He found himself stuck in town since his mother became ill, then died. He'd taken a provisional assignment at the community college, and he needed to get his mom's house ready to sell. Settling her small estate and his teaching job held him. *Just to the end of the semester*, he promised himself, *just until June.*

He didn't see his lanky reflection. His hazel eyes looked inward, trying to find his soul. Chestnut fuzz on his neck should have reminded him that his haircut was a week overdue.

A love interest would improve his situation, but he'd given up. He didn't date students, bad policy. The country club set was out. He didn't have the money, and he told himself they would not tolerate his political activism. He had a hazy notion that the stereotyping could work both ways, but he didn't dwell on it. He'd given up.

The hairdresser didn't remember her high school history, but she was cute. They met at a singles water-skiing picnic. Harv didn't have a boat, but he was in demand as an experienced driver on the small lake east of town. At six feet five, Harv was beyond the optimum size, but his skiing technique was good and he drove with care, never compromising safety.

Harv couldn't take the hairdresser's ex-boyfriend or the noise, dirt, and accidents of the weekend hydroplane races at Lake Isabella she insisted upon attending. They didn't date more than a few times. Before the hairdresser, Harv dated a flight attendant he met at the Bakersfield airport in the days when he left town every weekend, before his mother died.

His higher pay for teaching in the area went to the airlines. When the tule fog permitted planes to leave, he flew to San Francisco, San Diego, LA, anywhere with a more cosmopolitan atmosphere. The airline reassigned the flight attendant. There was no one at the moment.

He drove for a while, up into the hills, thinking about the call from his attorney. It was official. His attorney said he could legally dispose of the house and his mother's assets. Harv headed out of town, nowhere special. The pond looked like a good place to stop and walk. Maybe not. Alone with his thoughts, Harv didn't see a gray Cadallic slow and stop or the man behind the wheel take out a small pair of binoculars and look in his direction.

*   *   *

Across the road from the pond, Harv saw the Kern County Humane Society sign. An attendant opened the cyclone gate into the dog area and the barking intensified. The racket sent lightening bolts through Harv's head. He glanced at the rows of caged dogs and took a step back before he moved to follow the Humane Society worker. At the end of the row, another worker hosed the cages. Water and refuse swirled into the drains in the cement floor. Harv tried to calm the revulsion in his stomach from the sight and smell of animal wastes. He'd turned to leave when he saw her.

A black dog stood silent, calmly watching him. She had long tufts of tawny-highlighted fur circling her head and a couple tan toes on her right hind foot. Her black tail had long tan "feathers." A small patch of long tan hair sprouted from the middle of her chest. Harv stared at her. She bared her teeth.

"Great dog if you can't decide on long or short hair." The attendant laughed. "She's got both. Ugliest thing I've seen in a long time."

Harv continued to watch the dog, so the worker said, "She might look okay if you had her shaved. Give her a buzz cut. Take off all that long, brown stuff."

47

Harv's human companions hadn't worked out. When he left the pond and walked back to his truck, there it was across the road, the county animal shelter. He'd decided he had to change his life, but he didn't know why he went into the Pound.

"Why'd they bring her in?" he asked.

"Who?"

"I don't know. Her family. Why'd they bring her in? What's wrong with her?"

"Besides her looks? Just kiddin'. Between you and me, buddy, we put them down when the family brings them in. We picked up this one. She has a collar so she gets three days. Time's up tomorrow."

With her clumps of long hair protruding behind her jaws, she reminded Harv of a miniature lion who'd lost a fight. Harv moved closer. He looked into her intense, brown eyes. She growled.

"Probably not good with kids," said the attendant.

"That's okay. No kids."

"She probably ain't especially good with people either. I have to tell ya."

The dog turned her back on Harv when he touched the cyclone fencing of her cage. She hunched her hindquarters and took a dump right in front of him. Harv moved away a few steps. A white pit bull in the next cage lunged at him. Harv looked back at the quiet dog with bad manners.

"Reminds me of a few people I know."

"Hey, you some kind of nut? Want a dog to beat and torture? You're at the wrong place, bud."

"Nah, I need a friend. A no bull-shitting friend. Let's see if she'll tolerate me."

48

The attendant looked like he had a clever retort, but he swallowed it and pulled on heavy gloves. "Just a precaution. She hasn't bitten anyone that we know about." He swung the door wide and stepped aside. The dog watched every motion but made no move to bolt.

Harv squatted and offered the back of his hand for her to sniff. "Come on, girl. Come on. It's okay."

Her tail gave a slight motion. Harv stood up slowly. The dog looked from Harv to the worker and back, then she surveyed the whole enclosure. No escape. She came out a step at a time, gave Harv's hand a cursory sniff, circled behind him and leaned on his legs. She looked at the staffer from behind Harv and curled her lips.

"Impressive canines," said Harv. "You probably shouldn't have mentioned her last day."

"Likes you better than me. That's obvious. Got a leash?"

*   *   *

In the truck, the dog sat on the passenger seat and leaned against the door. When Harv reached to touch her, she pushed harder against the door.

"It's okay, girl. It's okay." Harv pulled a half-eaten energy bar from his pocket and offered her part of it. The dog gave him a look that Harv interpreted as, "What kind of dog do you think I am?"

He left the stale treat on the seat, and the dog ignored it. Harv's old feeling of malaise returned. "What was I thinking? A dog? A dog's going to solve things for me?"

Harv squeezed his forehead with his left hand as he drove. The dog relaxed. She carefully nosed the crumbly snack onto the floor and settled herself into the seat. Harv resisted the urge to pat her.

"I suppose you need a special diet?"

The dog seemed to smile at him. She allowed Harv to scratch her ear. They headed back to town and Harv's apartment. He told her his problems. In time the dog sat up, yawned and pawed at her window.

"Need some air? I'm not surprised. Couple of the women I dated said the same thing. You listened almost thirty minutes. That's pretty good."

Harv lowered her window four or five inches, and the dog jammed her nose through the opening. She stood on the seat with her hairy tail sweeping Harv's arm while she watched the road. Harv continued to talk.

"Since we're coming to my place, I should introduce myself. Harvey Leigh, Ph.D., History. My credential says I'm also qualified to teach physical education and English. Basically, I loved college, being a student. Stayed as long as I could. Loved Berkeley."

His dog shot him a glance that reminded him of one of his mother's looks. His mother, Fay, who never forgave his father for not becoming a rich enough oil man to enable his family to escape the Kern county oil fields. His mother could charm strangers but tore her family apart with her fierce temper, baiting insults and nagging. Fay loved her family, but she'd had no patience and few human interaction skills for the people closest to her. Harv replayed the time she disinherited him with words discharged for maximum kill, like exploding shotgun shells. *Okay, that's the last time. I know she wasn't herself then.*

She didn't mean it, he'd tell himself, but her venom stung. At the end, when she could barely speak, he told her he loved her. She managed to say, "I love you, too, Harv. With all my heart." They smiled and squeezed each other's hands. Harv kissed her forehead. He acknowledged the love but wished the relationship had been better.

He waved his thoughts away. His mother died seven months ago. *Well, I'm close to Del. We chose to emulate Dad, or what we remember of him.*

His sister, Del, a legal secretary in San Diego, rarely visited their mother while she lived. Harv took care of getting the will probated and preparing the house for sale.

The dog dozed. Harv realized he had been quiet when he startled her. "Enough of such thoughts. A few more blocks and we'll be home."

A woman with maroon hair and tattooed lipliner and eyebrows watered the planters at the entrance to Harv's apartment house. "This is not good," said Harv. The dog went on alert at his tone. She gave her lips a quick lick and looked around. "You'll have to stay here, girl. Landlady hates dogs."

Harv looped the rope leash through the door handle and left the dog sitting on the sidewalk beside the truck. His landlady watched him while she waved her hose in the direction of the plants. "No pets, Dr. Leigh. I'm not going to have any trouble with you, am I?"

"Trouble, Mrs. Stukey? No."

"That dog. You're not bringing a dog in here, Mr. Leigh."

Harv raised an eyebrow at his demotion. He wanted to say something like Do you see me bringing the dog inside, Mrs. Stukey? But why bait her? Instead he said, "Only stopped to pick up a few things. She's not going inside."

"See that it doesn't. You can't keep it. I'll be watching you. Remember your rental agreement."

"I just picked her up. We're going to pal around, have a drink or two, dinner. Who knows what might develop?" Harv gave Mrs. Stukey a wink and wiggled his eyebrows. His landlady scowled.

When he rented the apartment, she had warned him that she didn't approve of overnight lady friends. In a perverse way, the warning sounded promising, but there had been no overnight lady friends, to his dismay. Moving in with his mother was unthinkable, besides she'd needed the extra bedrooms for her health care aides.

Harv walked through the gate, grabbed his mail without looking at it and went up to his apartment. He sat at his computer, tapped out his two-week Notice of Intent to Vacate, and packed enough for the night and next day. Downstairs, Mrs. Stukey darted past him and rushed into her apartment on the first floor.

"Ah, Mrs. Stukey?" Harv frowned. He pushed his two-week notice under her door and went to his truck. He found his dog shaking water from her coat.

"What'd you do, growl at her?"

The dog sat up, front feet crossed in the air. Again, she seemed to smile.

"Well, it probably feels good even if the old crab didn't have cooling you off in mind." Harv walked the dog to the small patch of lawn. The dog rolled, sniffed and squatted. Harv heard a window open.

"That's going to burn a hole in the grass!"

"Not if you hose it right away, Mrs. Stukey. As you did my dog."

The window slammed. Harv stowed his gear and unfolded a small tarp to spread on the passenger seat for his wet dog. He didn't pay any particular attention to other comings and goings on the block or to the gray Cadillac down the street.

Linda Lanterman

Chapter 8

The Cadillac was an old model, going to rust, a two-door, long, heavy in the rear. The man in the driver's seat spoke into his cell phone, then listened.

"Yeah, an apartment complex. A landlady type talked to him. He must live here. Came out with a carry-on, like. Might be leavin' town.

"No, I toll ya.' No diggin.' Jus' walked around, poked at some things with his foot. Kicked some rocks. Stuff like that. Didn't look suspicious. Not like he was searchin' for anything."

"Hey, if he was callin' the cops why would he come out with a dog?"

"Sure I'll follow him."

"No, a funny lookin' mutt. Big enough. Not huge. Something you'd toss into the ring for the fighters to warm up on."

"I already toll ya. I never go out there. Jus' happened by when I seen this guy walking around real slow, lookin' at the ground."

*　　　*　　　*

Harv didn't think much about the man in the gray Cadillac. He saw the hard stare the guy gave him when he swung his truck in a U-turn, but Harv had other things on his mind as he headed for his mother's place.

He still thought of the house as hers. The For Sale sign pounded into the front lawn in anticipation of the court's action held the hope that Harv wouldn't have to deal with it much longer. Tonight, however, he was glad to have a place to stay with his dog. He would move out of his apartment tomorrow. If the house sold, he would arrange for escrow to close the first of June.

Harv parked in the driveway and sorted his mail. He found what he hoped for, the interview appointment with DeAnza College in Cupertino. He leapt from the truck with a little jig. His spirits began to improve. He noticed the wide streets of the old neighborhood where he grew up, the mature shade trees and green lawns, the City Park at the end of the street. His dog sniffed the air.

"Lucky," he said. How about Lucky?" The dog, unimpressed, watched him from the open door and scratched her stomach with her hind foot. "Guess not." Unaware of his gray shadow, Harv felt great.

A tall teen-ager bounced his basketball down the sidewalk. "Hey, Dr. Leigh. You got a dog!" The kid tucked the ball under his arm and adjusted a red tennis racquet case strapped over one shoulder.

"Yeah, Roy. Careful, I don't know how friendly she is. Doesn't even have a name. Just got her."

"How 'bout Nightmare?"

"No, she might take offense."

Roy tousled the dog's head before Harv could intervene. "Great dog, Dr. L. Kinda funny-looking but friendly." The dog's tail whipped back and forth in wide arcs. She took the young man's hand in her mouth in mock aggression.

"She scared the guy at the pound," said Harv.
The dog bumped the basketball away and began chasing it.

"Oh, oh. Don't want her to puncture it," said Harv as he retrieved the ball. "Want to play a little cage when I get this gear unloaded?"

"Really like to, Dr. L, but I'm overdue at home. Tennis gets all my spare time these days. Tennis and school work. Hey, you should come up to the tennis center with me some afternoon. Couple of new 'A' players. Sisters. Ranked juniors."

"Too young for me."

"Yeah, suppose so. Not too young for me. I hit with 'em now and then." Roy headed home after a final pat for the dog. "Later."

A free copy of the *Bakersfield Californian* with an invitation to subscribe lay rolled in a rubber band on the porch steps. Harv pushed it aside with his foot and pulled out his keys. "Your home will be in back," said Harv. "Nice fenced backyard, room for you to sleep under the porch. Hey!"

The dog pushed into the house when he unlocked the door, and there was no getting her back outside. Tomorrow, Harv told himself, knowing he'd already lost round one.

He settled in his old room, made the bed, then remembered he had no food. He was heading out when someone came up the steps and rang the bell.

A honey-blonde, twenty-something with sparkling blue eyes smiled at him. The braces on her top front teeth surprised him. She wore an English riding habit, minus the hat and riding crop. Her hair was pulled into a knot at the back of her head. She handed Harv his newspaper. Caught off guard, Harv dropped his gaze to the ground. The young woman wore tall, form-fitting boots and the skintight pants of a rider.

Geez, looks familiar. From where? A faculty member? Horse woman. Don't know any horse people.

"Oh, Dr. Leigh. Hi, I'm Amy. We, my aunt and I, saw lights — She asked me to check. Was Fay your mother?"

A student! A former student, maybe. "Fay, ah, yes, my mom." *A little older than most students.*

"Nice pants." *Bad. How could I say that?*

Harv felt blood rising in his face. Amy's smile changed. She cocked her head to one side. "Don't remember me, do you?"

"We've met. I know it. You look familiar."

"American History, last fall, Tuesday and Thursdays, six-thirty to eight, across from the Student Center. Didn't have the braces then."

"Of course, back of the second row. Amy! Amy, of course. An A student. The outfit. The outfit threw me. Come in."

"Got a B plus. A's in everything else."

"Oh." *Damn. Why couldn't I go with my gut instead of the percentiles? Nothing magic about numbers. Obviously deserved an A. Too damned hard-nosed.*

"You have company." Amy pointed to the dog sitting to one side of the door observing. "What's his name?"

"I don't have a name for her. Just got her today. Any ideas?"

"Hmm. Diverse background. Alert. Intelligent. Not the nervous type. Didn't bark at me. Can she bark?"

"Sure. I assume so. She has a loud yawn." Harv and his dog exchanged glances.

"Roy, from down the street, suggested Nightmare."

"How about something exotic like Singapore? No, too long. Gibraltar? Not Gibraltar. Xanadu, Quito?"

Harv threw in his own suggestions. "Venice? Troy? No, sounds masculine. What about Jakarta or Quetzalcoatl? Quetzalcoatl would be perfect, the feathered serpent of the Maya. San Jose has a big statue of Quetzalcoatl downtown. Fits this dog more ways than one."

"Fits her, but it's too long," said Amy.

The dog swung her head from one to the other.

"How about Quito or Jakarta, said Harv. What do you think?"

"Yes, Quito's better. Two syllables instead of three or more, easier to say. See if she likes it, Dr. Leigh."

"Harv. Call me Harv, please." He called his dog by her new name several times. Amy joined in. The dog bounded from one to the other, then rolled over and started racing around the house. Her toenails clicked on the hardwood floors. Quito slid and bumped into chairs, bounced off overstuffed furniture and raced upstairs and back.

"Looks like she likes the name," said Harv, but he watched Amy more than his new dog.

Amy laughed. "She's happy. Wants us to chase her."

"Not in the house." Harv tried to catch Quito on one of her passes, but she dodged him before coming to a stop. She crouched down on her front paws, ready to race away if he made another move to catch her. Harv put up his hands in surrender. "Ladies, may I suggest dinner?" Amy and Quito both tilted their heads and looked at Harv. *Dinner must be a magic word. This is good. This is good.*

"My aunt said to invite you to dinner, Dr. Leigh — Harv—if you were the one who turned the lights on.

Should warn you, though. She's heating up stew. Lots of boiled cabbage. Left over from yesterday. Not my favorite." Amy wrinkled her nose. "Maybe we could go somewhere simple or get take-out. I could tell Aunt Thora I need to help you with your new dog."

"Ah, sure. Great! Let's go out." *Very good. That was easy.*

"I'll go change and be right back."

Harv and his dog stayed on the porch and watched her go. "Sure you don't want to be called Lucky?"

Quito did not respond. Her body tensed. Harv followed her line of sight to a gray Cadillac.

Same guy that was across from the apartment. What's going on?

Harv watched Amy walk back to her aunt's, across the street and down a few doors, away from the Cadillac. Harv went inside, raced upstairs, found his overnight kit and pulled out his Right Guard, toothpaste and toothbrush. He thought a moment then decided he had time for a quick shower. Quito sat and watched from the doorway. She appeared amused.

*   *   *

Auntie Thora clapped her hands on her cheeks with joy when she learned Amy met Harvey Leigh. "Well, of course! It would be Harvey. I knew he came back. Teaches at the college. I can't believe I didn't think of him. You're perfect for each other."

"Auntie, I need to get changed. Fast!"

"Of course you do. Jump in the shower. I'll lay out your clothes."

Unable to decide, Aunt Thora put three outfits on the bed for Amy. As soon as Amy turned off the water, Thora started her chatter. Auntie had known Harv Leigh since he was a child.

"What a nice young man! Wasn't always sure how he'd turn out. Once I saw him wrestling another little boy on his front lawn. They were ten or eleven at the time. They tumbled around like nobody's business, until Fay came out and stopped them. Next thing you know they started laughing like best friends. Just like that." She snapped her fingers.

Amy accepted Thora's help and listened, although she pretended she wasn't. She wished her mom was still alive and could be sharing this moment, but Auntie was a good substitute.

*   *   *

Harv turned off the shower, reached for his towel and heard Quito downstairs barking. Angry barking, furious. He grabbed one of his mother's skimpy bath towels and wrapped it around himself. He dashed downstairs and found Quito on the couch under the living room window with her front feet on the windowsill. She shot a glance at Harv and turned back to the window. Her barking went into overdrive. Harv pulled the lace curtain aside to see a man hurry from the driveway to the gray Cadillac. Same man. "What the hell?" Harv opened the front door and raced onto the porch.

"Hey!" He stopped at the top of the steps when he remembered his bare feet and towel. Quito flashed by like a shadow. She tore after the man. She reached him as he opened the car's door.

"Ow!" The man kicked at her. "Shit!"

Harv gripped his towel and ran into the street. The man had his body halfway into his car, but Quito had the cuff of his pants. He sat up, tried to slam her with the door. Harv yelled. He didn't see the gun until he reached the Cadillac.

The ugly, black barrel pointed at Harv chest. He felt chilled, exposed. How could a small gun seem so huge?

"Call the mutt off!"

It took Harv a moment.

"Call her off, Buster, or she gets it."

"Quito! Quito! Come!" Quito jerked her head and tore away trouser fabric. She shook her head, let the material drop and went to stand by Harv. "Good girl. Good girl," said Harv with more than a touch of surprise and pride.

"What you doing to my truck?"

"Nothin,' ya big jerk. I was just lookin' at it. Thought I might get me one. I've a mind to sue you, lover boy."

A police siren wailed, and a patrol car rounded the corner. The gun disappeared. The man fumbled for his keys but couldn't get them out of his pocket in time. Harv suddenly seemed to remember his nudity, covered by a skimpy towel. Quito dashed for the open front door of her new home.

It took twenty minutes to sort out things with the patrolman. At first, he assumed Harv caused the disturbance, but 'Chuckie' Mandel and Officer Hastings knew each other. When Harv mentioned the gun, Chuckie said, "No gun." Chuckie refused a full search, however. Thought he should have a lawyer.

The officer said, "Since when don't you have a gun, Mandel? You got a license to carry."

"Watchin' the street. That's all. The guy's a nut. Look at him."

"Anyone see a gun?" The small cluster of neighbors shook their heads. The officer turned back to the characters in front of him.

"I did," said Harv.

"Besides you."

The neighbors standing at a distance snickered and made jokes. Officer Hastings didn't let Harv go until he had a formal statement. Hastings had attended a conference the past weekend and tried out his new dispute resolution skills.

Harv learned that Chuckie Mandel was a private investigator, but little else. The cop didn't appear to like the guy, but Hastings didn't seem to have any sympathy for Harv either.

*   *   *

Harv found Amy and Quito on his front porch. Amy had a smirk on her face. "Guess I missed something." She covered her mouth and nose with her hand and giggled.

"I, he…the cop…" Harv gestured wildly. "The guy in the gray car followed me, from my apartment. Can't understand it." Harv's face blushed crimson. "Need to get dressed. Be right out." He stubbed his toe going through the door.

Amy laughed with her hand up at her face. "Good idea," she said and turned to Quito. "Terribly underdressed, don't you think?"

Chapter 9

Jack Buggett waved off the waiter in formal dress serving honey-roasted squab on Spode china. He kept his salad and moved the blue cheese crumbles and walnuts to one side of the plate. He poked holes in the fresh pear slices with his fork before putting it down. Fancy spring greens littered the tablecloth. Jack scooped them back onto his salad dish with his right hand and nibbled a piece of his sourdough roll. He didn't touch the Napa Valley Chardonnay the wine steward insisted he must taste. The other guests at his table talked among themselves. After asking about Emma, they found it difficult to draw Jack into conversation and didn't try. They knew his wife lay dying in El Camino Hospital in Mountain View.

Thurston James' voice boomed from the podium. "Ladies and gentlemen, I conclude our awards this evening with special recognition for two of our founders, Jack Buggett and Travis Ping."

Waiters distributed after-dinner drinks or coffee to the guests in one of the San Jose Fairmont Hotel's smaller ballrooms. Jack watched the light's refraction from the massive crystal chandelier overhead.

"Jack! Jack, come on," said Travis Ping.

"What?" Jack looked at Travis.

"Thurston wants us up at the podium."

"What?" Jack looked over to Thurston James then back into the sparkling chandelier.

Travis went to Jack. "It's a special award, Jack. Just go up and say 'Thank you.' That's all we have to do." Travis helped Jack to his feet, shook his hand, pointed him forward and linked his arm in Jack's. Jack looked back. The people at his table rose and clapped, then others around the room.

Thurston spoke into the microphone. "Travis Ping runs the Hawaiian branch, as you know. Jack visited Honolulu a while back to help out Travis with all the new business. Jack and Travis are the guys, ladies and gentlemen. The men, you'll remember, who refused handsome bribes to look the other way when our container from Shanghai arrived in Honolulu with contraband. The container cleared US Customs, but good old Jack noticed a dummy bill of lading. Jack and Travis personally checked the load.

"Jack. Travis. You're either very smart guys or really dumb ones. Ha! Just kidding, ol' buddies. Come on up here and get your plaques and the hearty thanks of FG.

"Jack's detective work helped head off an international incident. The Chinese don't like to have their graves robbed or their national treasures stolen. No arrests yet, but Jack and Travis' quick action immeasurably enhanced the reputation of Fantasy

Geographica. Not to mention all the free advertising we received."

Later that evening Jack turned off Grant Road in Mountain View and into one of El Camino Hospital's parking lots close to the front entrance. He parked carelessly using two spaces. On the fourth floor, he walked down the hall of death to his wife's room. The hospital wanted to transfer her to a skilled nursing facility across the street, but Emma had so little time, the staff relented. Jack settled into the chair at her bedside. He thought she was asleep.

"The ring, Jack—Thank you."

"Ring?"

"Jade—ring."

All Emma's jewelry was at home or in their safe deposit box. The hospital didn't recommend patients wear jewelry under these circumstances. Jack gave Emma a jade disc set in gold for her birthday. He'd had it appraised and set at Ming's in Honolulu. His gift surprised her. He remembered she kissed him and hugged him through her tears. He remembered, too, how brave she was when she had to relinquish her rings a few months later when they both knew she would not be returning home.

"They recognize your good deeds?" Emma's voice fluttered. She didn't open her eyes.

"Gave me a plaque," said Jack.

Emma's eyelids struggled to open. The corners of her mouth tried to smile. She lifted a hand an inch or two. Jack held up the plaque for her to see, then put it down. She didn't waste words on a reply. She studied his face. He took her small hand in his big one, unaware of his tears. Emma died that night. Jack still held her hand.

*   *   *

In Pasadena, the director of the Pacific Asian Museum reported to the *Los Angeles Times* and to the police that a man had offered to sell him a priceless Chinese artifact. The individual said he had some limestone plates with bronze wire fasteners. He claimed the fragments came from the first stone armor ever found in China, from a burial suit from the tomb of Qin Shi Huang Di, Emperor from 221 to 210 BC. The man also showed the director an ancient jade button of more recent origin. "It was also a burial piece. I recognized it as one of a set of constellation buttons. The holes in the disc represent stars in a constellation. Each button has a unique pattern of holes that I believe represents a different constellation."

Director Stanley strode away. In his outrage, he failed to get much of a description of the man who had approached him on the street. When he cooled down, the museum director went to the *Times* to get the story out to art dealers and museums across the country. Law enforcement had a greater interest in the supposed thief, but no proof of a crime.

Chapter 10

Amy hung up the phone and saw Auntie's smug expression. *Oh, God. I say "yes" to a fourth date, a simple picnic, and Auntie's planning the wedding. Need to calm her expectations.*

Thora started to hum "Here comes the bride."

Sure, he's interesting, but Auntie gives me hives.

"How come they named him Harvey? Wasn't that someone's big white rabbit in a silent movie?"

"His father's name, dear. He's named after his father. And, by the way, they had 'talkies' when I was a girl.

"Can't imagine why I didn't think of him sooner. Well, I can. He didn't live at home. Had an apartment across town. Before she died, Fay told me he was back, teaching at the college. I simply forgot. Such a nice young man. Where you going tonight, a movie?"

"He bought take-out, Chinese." *I think we'll take Quito for a run after dinner and watch a video. I won't be late."

"Take those cookies I baked this afternoon. Going out Saturday, too?"

"I hope so." She smiled broadly, conceding victory to Auntie Thora. Amy stuffed six oatmeal raisin cookies into a plastic bag and headed out the door and down the street to Harv's. The sight of a police car in front of his house stopped her.

She approached slowly. She could see the officer and Harv on the front porch. Quito spotted Amy, stood up and barked a quick greeting. Harv waved her to come ahead.

She went up the steps and reached to pat Quito. "Hi. What's going on?"

"Couple teen-agers found part of a human skeleton near the Humane Society, ma'am. Dr. Leigh was seen in the area. We wondered if he saw anything."

"Oh, right, I read about it in yesterday's paper."

"Didn't notice anything out at the pond or the Humane Society. The only thing unusual about that day was Chuckie. I told Officer Sanchez about Mandel," said Harv. "The man in the gray Caddy who was across from my apartment and followed me over here. Someone called because Officer Hastings came out. He took a report."

"I saw Mr. Mandel, too, Officer. He parked down the street." Amy waved her hand to indicate the direction.

"Yes, we'd like to talk to Mr. Mandel. Let us know if you see him again, will you?"

The three of them shook hands. Harv wondered aloud if some of the neighbors felt disappointed to see the officer drive away without him. Amy laughed, but Harv scratched his head and looked at his shoes.

"I walked around the pond that day." Harv ran through the day again. "Didn't notice anything except some dead baby bass. I needed to sort out some things. Picked out Quito at the Pound. Went to my apartment. Noticed Chuckie across from my apartment, then here. Quito ripped his pants. I have no idea why he was there, or why the cops want to talk to him. Sanchez says they can't find him. Something's screwy."

"Bet it's about the skeleton," said Amy.

She found Harv distracted all evening. He was a crummy date. She hesitated when Harv asked her out the next night.

"Haven't been great company, have I?" Harv said as they strolled down the street to Aunt Thora's. "I'll do better. How about a picnic tomorrow?"

"Can Quito come?"

"Sure."

"Okay, then. I want to ask you about any contacts you have in the Bay Area, since you went to Cal. Search your brain for anyone I might contact, please. I'll need a job when the semester's over." Amy leaned over and kissed his cheek, turned quickly and opened the door.

"Oh. Yeah, sure." Harv looked blank as he watched her disappear into her aunt's house. It was not the evening he'd planned, either.

Saturday's picnic started much better. They drank Merlot from long-stemmed wineglasses and split a turkey-bacon club sandwich from Subway. Amy brought more of Auntie Thora's oatmeal raisin cookies. Quito waited for crumbs before eating the kibble Harv brought for her.

Without apology, Amy brushed her teeth with the help of a drinking fountain. She carried her toothbrush everywhere since she had the braces glued to her upper front teeth. Harv watched her half-amused, half-perplexed. They had not kissed, not a real kiss. He found himself staring at her lips. He wondered how it would feel to kiss her, but the fearsome wires on her teeth deterred him. One, or both of them could be wounded. He knew she read his thoughts. He was so obvious. He watched her eyes dance in the twilight. They stretched out on his Cal football blanket under a live oak in a quiet corner of the park and watched the sunset. Her head rested on his arm. She relaxed. He'd bring the Rutherford Hill Merlot again.

Right when things seemed so promising, Amy straightened and asked him about people she might contact in the Bay Area.

"Later. Lean back here." Harv saw her eyebrow take flight, but she returned his smile. Her eyes searched his. He waited. "I'm not sure how I going to do this either," he said.

They managed. Quito flopped down with a sigh, rolled her eyes and took a nap.

On the stroll back home, Harv searched his brain for someone to recommend in the Bay Area. He told her about his successful interview in Cupertino. "Don't have the contract yet, but they promised one. I could have flown home without the plane! Only problem is the high cost of living in Silicon Valley. That, and having a dog. I'd like it if you worked at DeAnza College too. I know where the placement office is." He squeezed her hand. "We could share a tiny apartment somewhere." His words hung in the air between them.

"My first priority is a decent job," said Amy pulling her hand from his.

"Wait a minute!" Harv startled Amy with his outburst. "There's Travis! Travis Ping. I think his parents must still live in Sunnyvale, unless they moved. His grandparents live in Hawaii. Anyway, he's one of the founders of Fantasy Geographica. The company does adventure trips for kids. For anyone, now. Adults, too.

"When I was in junior high and high school, I went on six trips led by Travis. Up to Bass Lake, a week hiking at Mammoth, sailing on San Francisco Bay, deep sea fishing off Catalina Island and gold panning on the Yuba River. I also went to Hawaii, but I missed a caving trip in the Southwest. Mom didn't go for that one. What great times! Even after college, I went over and helped out on some deep-sea fishing trips when he opened a branch office in Honolulu. He lives there, but I'm sure he has all kinds of contacts in the Bay Area. I'll shoot off an e-mail tonight."

At the door to Aunt Thora's Harv asked Amy about taking in a movie during the week. She hesitated. "I'd like to, but I have a paper due. Let me see how the studies go," she said.

"Next weekend, then?"

"Next weekend I need to drive to LA, for a quick visit with an old friend."

"Oh?"

"Would you like to come along? He's sort of like a father. A really nice old guy. I've never been to

73

Los Angeles. The freeways terrify me, all that traffic I see on the news. I envision myself driving around lost for days." She looked up at Harv.

The *father* and *old guy* parts tumbled in his thoughts, part relief and part anxiety. Yet Amy looked up at him with so much hope. She touched his arms. "I know it's a long drive, but I wish you'd come."

"Not that long of a drive." Harv rubbed his chin, then took Amy's hand and led her out of the circle of light at the front door. "I could be persuaded, I suppose."

Chapter 11

"I never could have found my way around this place," Amy said. "You navigate these freeways like you grew up here."

"I practically did. LA's not that far from Bakersfield," said Harv while he maneuvered from the fast lane across four lines of vehicles to get to an exit for another freeway.

Amy tried to remain nonchalant about her first trip to Los Angeles, but her head swung back and forth too often. She absorbed it all, palm trees, smog, billboards, the coastal hills, the traffic, people in other cars.

When they reached Argus Pritchett's home, a two-story barn of a house on a small lot in the La Brea section of town, it was a bit of a surprise to Amy. "I always thought I had a good sense of direction, but I'm hopelessly lost."

"You read the map. Told me when to turn."

"I don't think I could find my way home without help."

"Good thing we have each other."

As they opened the doors of Harv's truck, Argus strolled down the front walk, his arms and smile spread wide. Even Quito appeared enchanted. She'd jumped over Amy and tumbled out the truck first. She raced in circles on Argus' front lawn, rolled and squatted.

"See you brought the boyfriend and his dog. Come here and hug an ol' man's neck, little sister." Amy ran and hugged him. Argus swung her around and put her down.

"Whoa! That is a mouthful of wire, lady. When you said braces, I thought you meant a removable retainer."

They laughed and turned to Harv. He stood a few steps from his truck.

"Thought you two only met once. What's this bear hug business?" He put his hands on his hips in mock disapproval.

"I think Harv wants a hug too," said Amy.

"Happy to oblige." Argus held his arms wide to Harv who quickly stuck out his right hand for a handshake and offered a Rutherford Merlot with his left.

Argus turned to Amy "It's true we met just once, but we talk on the phone all the time. Don't we, gal?"

"He's my sounding board. But I don't call all the time."

"Called me at the office, no less. You should hear the rumors she started before I gave her this number." Argus winked at Harv.

Amy retrieved her purse and a jar of Aunt Thora's pomegranate jelly. Argus seemed pleased.

"Haven't had homemade jelly for a long, long time." He fingered the label decorated with hand-drawn pomegranate blossom and looked up at Amy. "Be sure you thank her for me. And thank you."

He looped his arm over Amy's shoulder. "Nuff chatter. Come in. Come in. I got the barbecue ready to go. You like baby back ribs? Make my own sauce, passed down from my grandmother's grandmother."

Argus proved his ability as a chef. "World's best sauce," he said. "Got it from my first cousin's Georgia grandmother." Later it was from his daddy's Uncle Ted, then from Sue Ellen of an obscure connection.

"I wonder what's going on with this recipe, don't you, Harv?"

Argus laughed. "I took a pinch from everyone, rolled all their secrets into my own recipe."

They ate in the trellised backyard. Even Amy ate a few tasty, messy ribs.

"Big on rabbit food, I see," said Argus as he watched Amy with her salad.

They ate an early dinner and limited the wine. Argus suggested they spend the night. "You can each have your own bedroom and bath. Dog will be fine out here."

Amy and Harv planned to drive back that night. Amy said her aunt expected her. It was true this time.

Argus fixed a huge plastic plate of food, covered with foil, for Aunt Thora. He shook his finger at Quito. "Don't you go sneaking into that bag. Too many of those spicy ribs'll make you sick." Quito wagged her tail and licked her lips.

"That's going to feed us for the rest of the week," said Amy. "Auntie loves ribs, and it's a big change from the boiled dinners she fixes."

In a private moment with Amy, Argus said, "Seems like a nice young man."

Amy gave him a wrinkled nose smile, but her giggle and the color rising in her cheeks gave her away. "He is nice, but I'm not ready for anything serious. Neither is he. We're going water skiing, by the way. I haven't told him I'm pretty good, been around ski boats and fishing boats all my life. My parents rented a cabin at Lake Coeur d'Alene every summer."

Argus rubbed his chin then raised an eyebrow. Amy kept talking. "We'll have to see what develops in the Bay Area when this semester's over. First of all, I'll have to find work so I can finish my education."

When Argus had a chance to talk to Harv, he assumed a fatherly tone. "She's a quick study. Has lots to learn but plenty of brains and good sense." Argus pointed his finger for emphasis. "As her self-appointed guardian, I say to you: Don't mess with her."

Harv felt the force of Argus' expression. He saw the intensity in his eyes, then a quick change back to a twinkle of good humor. The flash of warning stayed with Harv. He wanted to protest, but the moment dissolved. He had no other opportunity.

They said their good-byes with another bear hug between Amy and Argus. Harv shook hands and raised his left hand in surrender, or a pledge. He wasn't sure which.

Chapter 12

Treasure Williams, Argus Pritchett's first cousin, came to Amy's rescue. She had a big home on Magellan Drive in the Montclair section of the Oakland hills. Argus called her and after some arm-twisting, she agreed to rent a room. Trez was a nursing supervisor at Highland Hospital in east Oakland. She urged Amy to take a nurse's aide position. Highland had openings, but Amy worried.

She tried to overcome her aversion to the sights and smells of the hospital, but the day she returned her application she almost became a casualty herself. A man and a woman delivered to the congested emergency room entrance from a car-truck collision on 35th Avenue caused the problem. Amy hyperventilated at the sight of a blood-soaked blanket over a body on the gurney. She tried to brace herself on a parked car. She couldn't breathe. A passing nurse caught her, sat her down on the walkway and yelled for assistance.

Amy suffered a flashback to the emergency room in Spokane. All the grim details of the night her parents died flooded over her.

Trez relented. "Pay isn't that great, and it's tough work. Why don't you go over to Cal and talk to someone in Student Aid? Maybe you could get by with a scholarship and a part-time job."

*   *   *

Amy fell in love with Cal. She spent a couple days wandering the Berkeley campus before her appointment with Admissions. She visited the Student Union and sat down for lunch and conversation with total strangers. The campus promised rigorous physical conditioning. She saw she would have to pay attention to building locations when she scheduled her classes.

She went to the top of the Campanile and hiked up to the Greek Theater. The scent of the eucalyptus trees reminded her of her grandmother's cough drops. She found the smell refreshing and friendly. Tall pines added their elegance. Green vegetation and flowers thrived in Berkeley's rich soil. When the fog rolled through the Golden Gate, San Francisco Bay moderated the climate and cooled the hills with moist caresses and mystery. How had she lasted in dusty Bakersfield for a whole year?

She wandered into Moses Hall, the old Eshleman Hall, and found the charming library on the second floor. She learned the building once housed the *Daily Californian.* She checked out the reading rooms of the Bancroft Library and dropped in on a lecture in Wheeler Auditorium until she realized it was Economics 1A. "Guns and butter" drove her back out the door before she found a seat. She earned an A in economics at Washington State, but she didn't want to sit through it again.

She got lost in the basement of Dwinelle Hall. When she returned to the Wheeler Auditorium at the end of the day, she caught a lecture on political philosophy. A visiting professor from the Sorbonne captivated her with his theories of sovereignty and national power. She decided to add more political science to her class schedule. Her preview of the campus helped her impress the people in Admissions the next day.

Transcripts in hand, she sought admission as an upper division student. The Admissions Office encouraged her, laid out the formal application process and sent her away with hope. Amy made an appointment to talk to someone in Financial Aid. The fees and her living expenses represented her largest obstacle. She had no idea an attorney in Spokane was looking for her.

*   *   *

Trez liked the skinny white woman. She had a good attitude and seemed eager to learn, even if she was faint-hearted around sick people. Both women liked Starbucks Coffee.

After her day at Admissions, Amy came home with steaming coffee for Trez, before she had to leave for her evening shift.

"Glory be, sweet thing. Sit down and chat a minute."

Amy needed no encouragement to tell Trez about her day. Trez had her degree from UCSF, in nursing, but she had taken some courses on the

Berkeley campus. When Trez could get a word in, she said, "What do you plan to wear?"

"To wear?"

"To the interview."

Amy thought a moment. "Auntie took me shopping and bought the dress with the rose pattern, yellow roses on a black background. What about it?"

Trez ran her tongue over her teeth. "Let me think. I have a black linen jacket might not be too big on you. How 'bout shoes? Have black shoes?"

Amy dashed to her room and opened her closet. She checked a pair of black leather low heels and brought them out. "Kind of scuffed," she said.

"Little polish will take care of that. Let's try my jacket. People who give out money like to give it to those who look like they don't really need it. Course, it's Cal. You never know."

Trez thought a moment. "Think we should go with the general rule. Let's make you look like a law student. When do those braces come off?"

"Another week." Amy's shoulders sagged. "The dentist in Bakersfield suggested I get my nose fixed, too. I can't afford it. Do you think I need to get my nose done? He made me feel terrible."

"Don't you touch that nose! It's perfect!" Trez's voice rose. Her hands went to her hips. She glared at Amy. "Why on earth would a dentist be talking about a nose job? Argus said your teeth were okay, too. I understand why you made yourself undesirable, but those wires are downright scary, child. Nothing we can do before your appointment, so forget them."

Amy thought with her hand over her mouth and nose. She pulled a red blouse from the closet. "Maybe I should wear something bright to make an impression."

"Don't wear red at Cal," said Trez. "Stanford color. Wear red during Big Game Week and everyone will yell, 'Take off that red blouse!' They will! Any blue in your wardrobe?"

Amy pulled out a blue dress, lighter than Cal blue, more like UCLA blue, but it complimented her eyes. Amy slipped it over her head. Trez held the black jacket for her to try. She hauled Amy to the full-length mirror on the bathroom door. Trez grinned.

"Uh huh! That's the look we want."

Amy turned round and round. "I look like a law student. I do." Up went the hand over her mouth and nose as she laughed.

"Forgive me, child, but there is one more thing. You must stop with the hand."

Amy looked bewildered. "The hand?"

"Between now and next Thursday, you are going to lose the hand business." Trez put her hand up to her face the way Amy did. Amy blushed. Trez hunched her shoulders and shuffled around exaggerating Amy's mannerism. Little frown lines appeared on Amy's forehead. Her lip quivered.

"Don't get weepy on me, little sister. I'm telling you how it is. You can change it. You're a lovely woman. You know what you do? You catch someone staring at your braces, looking at you sideways, you look 'em right in the eye and hold on to them with your stare." Trez demonstrated. "You want to ease the tension a bit, say something like, 'Makes kissing hell."

Amy laughed. Her hand came up, but she forced herself to drop it. "It does, I can tell you."

Trez pointed at her and cocked her head. "See there. That's confidence. You're learning already." Trez wrapped an arm around Amy's shoulder. They stood before the mirror studying Amy's reflection.

"Nice," said Amy.

"Damn straight. Ask for a hundred fifty thousand."

"What!"

"Tell 'em you're going on to law school."

Amy laughed. She didn't cover her face. "I have to repay it. The money's not free."

Trez dipped her chin as she watched Amy in the mirror. "Wonder how Dr. Harvey Leigh will react to your new look?"

"Oh, I think he kind of liked the skin-tight riding pants I had on when we first met."

*   *   *

Amy sailed through her interview with the man in Financial Aid. The problem was the money. Half way through, a fast mental calculation told Amy she couldn't make it on what Cal offered. College tuition would be rising. Every issue of the *Daily Californian* carried news of California's budget deficit and its impact on the University system. She swallowed, smiled and forced enthusiasm she no longer felt.

Amy dragged into the house in Montclair, trailing Trez' jacket. Trez called from the master suite upstairs, "How your interview go?"

"Fine."

Amy could tell Trez didn't like the sound of that. Trez came right down to the living room half-dressed.

"How can you have a fine interview and look so sad?"

"Good interview. Not enough money."

"Hey, we'll find a way. Don't you worry." But Trez was worried. Amy heard it in her voice.

"Almost forgot. Your auntie called. Said it was urgent. Chin up, now. Don't want to worry her."

Linda Lanterman

Chapter 13

Amy's call to Aunt Thora and then to Spokane was good news. Amy's father had an additional life insurance policy his attorney found when he reviewed the file before destroying it.

"You didn't know about it?" he said in a voice a little high, Amy noticed.

"No," said Amy. "You didn't know about it either?" Coldness seeped into her words. "You were the executor."

Trez raised her eyebrows and held out both hands in a silent expression of *What?*

Amy scribbled *$10,000 ins. policy.* She repeated "Uh-huh" a couple of times.

Trez's eyes narrowed. Amy's father died more than three years ago. Trez grabbed another pencil and wrote *penalties and interest???* Amy looked up at her. Trez gave her a quick nod.

"Well, certainly. I do appreciate your efforts to reach me, but you had Aunt Thora's number. She hasn't moved. You couldn't make two phone calls? Amy held the phone away from her ear. The attorney wasn't loud. He was long on excuses. Amy moved her fingers and thumb in a talk-talk motion. Trez rolled her eyes and looked cross.

Now the attorney sounded wounded. Amy put her hand over her heart and glanced heavenward. Trez circled *penalties and interest* three times.

"Yes, I'm getting along. Finishing my education. About to get engaged.

"Thank you. He's an attorney, too. Like you."

"Yes, one. Where's this money been all this time? I'm thinking about penalties and interest."

"I see. No, I don't think there should be any legal fees at all. Don't you agree? I mean, *you* managed the estate." Again, Amy held the phone out from her ear, then put it closer. "I wouldn't know if Dad forgot to mention the policy to you or not, would I?" After another pause, she spoke again. "Registered Mail. Yes. With a full accounting. Can I call you back tomorrow? I'm late for my date."

"Yes, good-bye."

Trez pulled a bottle of Cook's Champagne from the bottom of the refrigerator. "Engaged to a lawyer? Date? The sweet thing lies like a rug. Imagine that."

"I'm going to make it," said Amy. "I can finish school! I'm calling Argus." After she talked to Argus, she called Harv.

*   *   *

Mai Ip was one of the first people Amy met at Cal. "Mai is a campus activist," Amy said to Trez when she introduced her fellow student. "She drinks green tea and carries signs in Sproul Plaza."

Mai fanned her hand at Amy. Trez ignored Amy's attempt at humor. "Nice to meet you, Mai. You grow up around here? Have we met?"

"I attended Berkeley High and was active in speech and debate. Did you ever judge any of the tournaments? You look familiar to me, too. Amy said you were on the Oakland school board."

"That's it, I bet. I think I remember you. A speech to inform. I seem to remember that it was about the conditions in orphanages in China. Is that right?"

"You have a good memory, Trez. Yes, the orphanages but especially the deplorable educational conditions for poor children in rural China."

"Mai went to Shanghai last year as part of her Asia Studies project, Trez."

"Did you get out into the countryside?" asked Trez.

"Yes, for about two weeks. I know that isn't much, but I speak Mandarin. My great-grandfather was a merchant in Shanghai. He sent his sons here. They were the lucky ones. We could find no trace of the family or my aunts. They disappeared during the Japanese occupation in the 1930's."

Trez put her hands in her lap and shook her head. "What stories hide from you. What painful stories."

"I am lucky to be in this country and at Cal. Amy and I are thrilled every moment we are on campus. Think of the education we are getting! That's what makes us such good friends. We recognize how fortunate we are."

*   *   *

In the Bay Area, Amy didn't see as much of Harv as she hoped. They water-skied at the Berkeley Aquatic Park a couple of times with some of Harv's friends. Harv made points when he asked Amy, and not the boat's owner, to drive the boat when he skied. However, Cupertino and Berkeley proved farther apart than either realized.

The heavy traffic made the trip a nightmare during peak periods. And, there was the time Amy surprised Harv and arrived on the DeAnza campus early for their evening of dinner and a concert at Flint Center. She'd forgotten how silly some freshmen women could be.

She anticipated that Harv's students liked him. He was good-looking. He knew his subject. He was a tough grader, but he made lectures interesting.

Amy sat at a table in the student center and opened Thucydides' *Peloponnesian War,* required reading for her political philosophy course. The discussion at the closest table floated over her, abstract sounds, almost.

Suddenly the sounds made sense. The three co-eds discussed what it would be like to sleep with Dr. Harv Leigh. Amy's book suddenly sprouted brown droplets on the pages as she choked on her coffee. She recovered, mopped up and listened in dismay to the attractive young women. The fighting between Athens and Sparta could wait a little longer while Amy covertly surveyed the young women.

The students wore what she thought of as "expensive casual" outfits. She considered their hair and make-up and decided to call it "studied perfection." She thought she was fine until she realized she had her hand over her nose and mouth. She pulled it down, flattened her fingers on the table and took several deep breaths.

Harv noticed the co-eds before he saw her. When he did see her, Amy felt the young women's eyes. Unaware of the undercurrents, Harv introduced her to his students as "my friend, Amy Roth." Amy kept what she'd overheard to herself.

*   *   *

"Listen, child. If he's going to succumb to that kind of thing, it's better to find out now. Didn't you tell me he never dated students? Why would he start?"

"You didn't see them, Trez. Pretty, I mean, really pretty. Perfect clothes, perfect hair, perfect faces."

"Don't you have a paper due tomorrow? You better work on your studies and forget the things that *might* go wrong."

Amy's lower lip jutted. Trez relented. "Idle talk, little sister. High school stuff. Everything will work out." She crossed her fingers behind her back while she patted Amy's shoulder.

*   *   *

They didn't spend hours on the phone. When they talked, Harv told her about Quito and his classes.

"So far, so good on my evaluations. Dr. Ralph, likes me, so does the administration. Haven't made any enemies. The Academic Senate's Standards Committee isn't bad, but the tennis team takes a lot more time than I anticipated."

Amy listened to every word. If Harv included her in his future plans, she heard no clues.

She'd mapped out a schedule to graduate in two semesters, plus two summer sessions. She and Harv saw each other when time and distance permitted. Amy had not met Harv's friend, Travis Ping. Travis lived in Honolulu, but Harv introduced her to Travis' parents the first time Amy visited Silicon Valley. The Pings graciously offered Amy the use of a tiny studio apartment behind their old farmhouse in Sunnyvale. "It'll force us to clean it out," Mrs. Ping told her.

Tract houses surrounded their place, but they loved their old house on a quiet Sunnyvale cul-de-sac where the family orchard once grew. The Pings met at Cal, and they took on the mission of fostering the romance of another Cal couple. The arrangement solved both ethical and monetary problems for Amy.

She'd thought about it, but she had not slept with Harv. She didn't like the idea of jumping into bed with someone, even a person she cared about, without some idea of where the relationship was going. Harv didn't press, and she didn't let herself care too much.

Harv never said he loved her. Frustrating as the uncertainty was, Amy was glad he hadn't. The words came too easily for many guys. Neither she nor Harv seemed willing get carried away. They kept it light, no pressure, at least on the surface.

All the same, when Argus visited from Los Angeles, he saw the sparkle in Amy's eyes when she told him about Harv.

"Trez, I think this young woman's in love."

"Doesn't know it, if she is. You heard her."

"Oh, I know. Doesn't talk the talk. But she's walking the walk." Argus and Trez laughed. Amy looked from one to the other.

"Think you're so smart. You two don't know anything. Gotta get to class."

She stood. Blood rose in her cheeks. She tried to roll her eyes and appear nonchalant. She failed. But, her relationship with Harv was strained at that moment.

Amy had not seen Harv for almost two months. He called, but she put him off. It had started on a rainy Saturday. She and Harv strolled from the Stevens Creek Theater complex in San Jose and met Harv's department chairman and his wife.

"Dr. and Mrs. Ralph, you remember my friend, Amy Roth?"

"Certainly we do. Good evening, Amy," said Mrs. Ralph. Dr. Ralph smiled and added his "Good evening."

The men went for their cars while the women waited.

"I understand, Amy, but I was so sorry you couldn't attend the California History Center reception two weeks ago." Mrs. Ralph turned to watch an approaching car and did not see Amy's surprise. "I specifically told Harv to invite you because part of the new exhibit features some of Arthur Samish's personal papers." She turned back to Amy. "You know, California's most notorious lobbyist?"

Amy opened her mouth, but no words formed. Mrs. Ralph returned her gaze to the arriving cars. "The History Center is the old Triton Museum, a charming, historic house on campus. A delightful place for receptions. We had wonderful hors d'oeuvres. Your studies are important, but I knew you would find the exhibit interesting."

"When was it? I didn't know anything about it. Harv didn't mention it."

"Saturday, the fourth of April. It was a weekend so I thought you could attend. Not too long, four to six in the afternoon. Fancy finger food. Harv didn't mention it? Oh, my. He attended. Alone. Oh my. He said you had a paper due."

"I'm a poli sci major. I always have papers due." Amy heard her voice rise and tried to bring it under control. She thought she should make light of the whole thing, but she couldn't. The best she could do was, "Guess Harv and I need to talk."

Harv tried to apologize. And tried. And tried.

"Don't make my decisions for me," said Amy.

"Will I see you next weekend?"

"No, I have a paper due. Two of them, in fact. Maybe three."

"Amy,—"

Even though it was late and wet, Amy picked up her car at the Pings and drove back to Montclair.

It was two months before they dated again, but the spontaneity disappeared from their relationship.

The press of finishing her course work didn't help. In August Amy finished the last of her classes, and the weight lifted only to be replaced by another problem.

"I have one more interview scheduled at the Placement Office. I have to tell you, Harv, they've been disappointing so far." Amy couldn't disguise the discouragement in her voice as she spoke into the receiver. "I can go right to work in office management or legal research. That's what I did with less than half the college education!"

"Mmm."

"Harv?"

"What?"

"Don't know anyone in the Governor's office, or a Senator or Congressperson, do you?"

"Thought you wanted to work in the non-profit sector, not politics."

"I do, but I don't have any political connections. Everything seems to be who you know rather than what you know."

"Have you explored anything down this way? Cupertino, Sunnyvale or San Jose?"

"Not yet, but I will."

"Amy, promise you'll not accept anything until you look down here."

She beat back the urge to ask, *Why, Harv?* At last she smiled.

*   *   *

Harv had mandatory faculty meetings at DeAnza in late August, the day Amy completed her last exam and petitioned for graduation from Cal. They planned to celebrate that evening, however, with dinner at the Claremont Hotel. She didn't know that Harv had arranged a surprise party.

Amy met Harv's sister, Del, for the first time. Del placed an orchid lei of tiny purple and white dendrobiums over Amy's head and kissed her on the cheek. "A lei is more fun than a corsage," she said with a nod of her head at her brother.

Aunt Thora came from Bakersfield, Argus from Los Angeles. The Pings came and Amy's friend Mai. Aunt Thora seemed a bit standoffish at first, but the Pings and the cousins, Argus and Trez, overwhelmed her with their warmth and charm. The champagne helped, too.

Trez proposed a toast. "Over the space of the three semesters Amy spent at Cal she buried herself in her studies. She worked hard. Cal isn't easy." Here Trez stopped and looked for agreement. Auntie Thora looked very pleased. The Pings nodded. Harv kept his warm, hazel eyes on Amy. Trez continued. "She wanted to finish on schedule. She wanted good grades. To Amy." Trez raised her glass. "You've done it all."

Amy beamed, then she stood, her champagne flute in hand. "I could not have done it without the support and love each of you has given me. Thank you."

She raised her glass to each person in turn. Amy came to Harv last. Although she didn't intend it, she paused longest for Harv. Trez and Argus exchanged glances. Auntie chuckled and cleared her throat.

Amy felt as bubbly as her champagne, proud of herself and ready to enjoy the evening. When Aunt

Thora asked about her job search, Amy laughed it off and refused to consider anything that might spoil the mood.

Argus presented her with a tiny cell phone and a year's worth of calls. "The latest technology," he said. Aunt Thora gave her a gold chain with beautiful star sapphire that her husband had given to her fifty years ago. Regis Clifford and his sister, Julie, sent a note of congratulations and a Clifford Harness Racing check for a hundred dollars.

"Mad Money," said Aunt Thora. Martha sent her a card and red silk scarf. "Red? Should be blue and gold," said Aunt Thora. Amy shot her a glance, but this time everyone at the table agreed with Auntie. "Bright," said Thora.

The Pings presented Amy with a lifetime membership in the Cal Alumni Society. Trez gave Amy an index card on which she'd written *Tuesday, 2:30 p.m.* and an office number at Oakland City Hall.

"I know you're an alternate for the Legislature's Internship Program, but that's not a sure thing. This is an appointment to talk about a three-month internship in the mayor's office."

Amy sat up straight. "Trez!"

"Doesn't pay much of anything, but in experience. And, you have to show up to the interview.

"Trez, How? How?"

"Copied a couple of your professors' letters of recommendation, added mine and one from Argus here. You should get it." Trez tucked her chin in and looked over her reading glasses. "Called in a couple favors from my days on the school board."

Amy leaped to her feet. She hugged Trez, then everyone around the table.

"One more thing." Trez handed Amy a gift-wrapped box. "Mai and I went in on this. We kind of thought it would be fun."

Color rushed up Mai's neck to her cheeks. "Hope you like…It was Trez' idea," she said as her courage floundered.

"It was Mai's idea," said Trez "and a good one."

Amy opened the box and up flew both hands over her mouth and nose. Seemed like she hadn't done that in more than a year. Her hands covered an embarrassed, delighted laugh. She slowly withdrew a black lace slip, black stockings and a skimpy, black lace bra. Aunt Thora frowned, swallowed, then tried to get into the spirit of things. The black thong panties pushed Thora over the edge. She knocked over her water goblet and reddened more. Amy quickly stuffed the black lace back in the box and thanked everyone. "This is better than a birthday!"

*   *   *

Amy and Harv lingered after the others left. They strolled down by the tennis courts, then back inside the huge, landmark hotel.

"Amy, I have some good news."

"You got tenure?"

"Well, no. Have to teach another two years before I'm eligible. I won an all expense paid trip to Hawaii, for two."

"Really? How?"

"At the market. It happened automatically, every time I used my club card. The Safeway near my apartment. Did I tell you I crewed on several deep-sea fishing trips with Travis when I was at Cal and after I graduated?" Oh, man, I'm so excited. Travis said *Lola's* on the Big Island."

"Lola?"

"The Fantasy Geographica boat. Ever been deep-sea fishing? He says we can use it if he has nothing scheduled. It's been slow lately. Isn't that great?"

"Um. I've never known anyone whose won something like this. When will you be going?"

"Have to go between now and the end of January. What I want to talk to you about—Come with me?"

Amy hesitated.

"Amy, please. You're the only person in the world I want to go with."

"Really? Oh." Her eyes darted as if a computer in her brain couldn't process the information.

"Say yes."

"When? My job—The internship, if I get it. I need to think."

"It's only a week. We could go over the Christmas holidays. You know you could go."

"It would save me from Aunt Thora's lutefisk at Christmas."

"Lukefish?"

"Loot-uh-fisk. Norwegian lye fish. God-awful, slimy mess. Scandinavian tradition. She has it shipped from Minneapolis, special."

"Amy, about going to Hawaii — Will you come with me?"

"I guess so." Amy's smiled but a touch weaker than Harv anticipated.

"What is it?"

"I want to go. It's a wonderful opportunity. I just need to think."

"Tell me, Amy. What is it?" Harv's mind raced. *Tactical error, old boy. Should have told her I loved her first, Hawaii second. Now I'll sound insincere.*

"It's awkward, embarrassing, Harv, but I need to know."

Harv said nothing. He waited, cold with apprehension.

Chapter 14

In Sunnyvale, on a Friday, seven weeks after Emma Buggett's death, Fantasy Geographica laid off two of its five founders. Jack Buggett and Travis Ping didn't see it coming. The three-man majority mentioned the 9/11 terrorist attacks and the subsequent drop in bookings. Their reasoning challenged logic after all the company had overcome, but they cut staff at the Sunnyvale headquarters and closed the Hawaiian offices. A secretary in Honolulu and one in Kona continued on the payroll, part-time, working from their homes.

Fantasy Geographica hung Jack and Travis out to dry quietly, no press release, no explanation that made sense. Over the next three months, Jack Buggett lost his last tatters of sanity quietly, without a word.

His partners laid him off and cut his severance pay to eight weeks. Too late, he saw all the entangled pieces, the pattern that was no pattern. Steel cables drew around him. He felt his heart shrink. His lungs seemed to collapse, then everything turned red.

He appeared to function. Routine matters, his conversations seemed completely normal, but he would find his mind intermittently in surprising places. He lost his befores and afters, the connections.

*   *   *

Jack's windshield wipers worked to clear hard, cold rain from his windshield. He thought he recognized Thurston James' black Mercedes at the Lion and Compass Restaurant in Sunnyvale. He pulled into the lot and stared at the small Fantasy Geographica sticker that glistened on the Mercedes' rear bumper. Jack and Thurston once taught in the same middle school. Jack had no plan. He remembered nothing, only red.

The valet parking attendants didn't remember anything. A waitress said she saw a man talking to someone through an open passenger door, then get into the car. The witness could not describe either person. She couldn't tell Sunnyvale Public Safety if the driver was a man or a woman. Public Safety did place Thurston James at the Lion and Compass. He disappeared. They had his car, and the bartender identified James from his picture.

Jack strangled Thurston James with his hands, the hands that each could span half a basketball. The notice of termination of Jack's retirement benefits lay on his living room floor. Two fingers of Scotch rested in an Old Fashioned glass on Jack's coffee table. He kept a stocked bar, but Jack rarely drank, and only wine, when he did. Jack remembered nothing but silence and swirls of red clouds.

He put the body in his tub, shoes up against the wall, head at the drain. He slit Thurston's throat, went to bed while his partner's blood drained into the sewer.

Rain continued into the morning. The weather was perfect for a fire in the fireplace. After breakfast of Fruit Loops and lukewarm Sanka, Jack went to his garage for a piece of three-quarter inch plywood and his power saw.

What Jack and Emma had saved on their two-bedroom house in Sunnyvale, they'd spent on a 48-foot Beneteau sailboat moored in Alviso. In spite of the choppy seas and the threatening weather, Jack sailed San Francisco Bay each morning the third week in November. Piece by piece, Thurston James joined the underwater community of the bay.

*   *   *

"Oh, Mr. Buggett, I didn't realize you were home. I would have rung the bell," Rita Johnson said as she let herself into Jack's house. She carried her cleaning supplies in a bucket in one hand and stooped to pick up her vacuum cleaner with the other. She cleaned Jack's house once a month.

"It's fine, Rita. Come on in. I should have called to let you know I'd be home today.

"By the way, I cut my foot when I dropped a bottle of after-shave in the bathroom. Cleaned up best I could, but be careful. Might be some glass splinters."

"Don't worry, Mr. Buggett, I'll give your bathroom extra special treatment."

"That's great, Rita. Oh, something else. I'm leaving for Baja tomorrow morning. Be gone four months. I have a check here for you. For the time I'll be gone. Let yourself in as always. Lock up, when you leave. I want you to keep things going. Flush the toilets. Make sure nothing's amiss.

"Anyone asks, you don't have a clue. Got it?"

"Certainly, Mr. Buggett." Rita glanced at the check. "And, thank you. That's very generous."

*   *   *

Jack nosed his boat, *Avenger,* under the Golden Gate. Past the Farallon Islands, he plotted his course for Hawaii, not Baja. His memory of the trip held only red sunsets, red dawns, red seas.

When Sunnyvale Public Safety questioned Rita, she told the officer that Mr. Buggett said he would be gone four months and that he seemed distracted.

"Strange," she said. "He complimented me on my red dress."

"How's that?"

"It was odd. I wore a green-striped blouse and a tan skirt that day, the last time we talked."

*   *   *

Fantasy Geographica, a low-tech company, mimicked the high-tech rise of so many dot coms in Silicon Valley during the eighties and nineties. The founders started with nothing and became millionaires.

Seventeen years ago, five Stanford friends started the company with no capital, no facilities, nothing but daring bravado and charm. Three of the five taught junior high school, Travis Ping, Jack Buggett, and Thurston James. The other two, Howard Pugh and Hal Veil, business majors, worked in marketing in the computer industry. Pugh worked at Tandem, Veil at Intel. The young men drew up a business plan and a budget. The five sought out venture capitalists but received no funding. They refined their pitch and continued to skimp by.

The company began with school kids, adventure trips for boys during the summers and spring breaks. They would arrange a trip whenever they could pull something together: a borrowed ski cabin, special permit backpacking into national forests, rented boats for water skiing, rafting, fishing, gear for rock climbing. They taught the kids leadership skills, esprit de corps, self-confidence and clean fun. In the early days, the founders did everything.

Fees covered costs, things like gas, transportation and food. Profits didn't exist for the first three years, but they built a loyal client base. Word spread. They stored their small inventory of tents, and gear in Travis Ping's parents' garage and the tiny studio at the back of their property. No one worried about liability or litigation.

Jack Buggett had special talents in motivation, storytelling and organization. He could put a week's trip together in an afternoon, a little longer if it involved the National Park Service or travel out of state. Kids particularly wanted to go on the trips Jack led. Two or more founders might lead larger groups, but the optimum size to build the kids' self-assurance and leadership turned out to be five or six. As the company grew, things changed.

The partners incorporated after five years, and Fantasy Geographica took off. The founders devoted themselves to the company full time. Hal Veil earned his MBA. Profit became the number one goal. Now that they didn't need capital, venture capitalists approached them. Fantasy Geographica added adventure trips for adults. Their earliest clients, now college students or recent graduates, willing to work between semesters for minimum pay, became new guides for the kids. Fantasy Geographica hired a staff of professional guides and used outside contractors for the more unusual trips.

On the company's tenth anniversary, Travis Ping moved to his home state, Hawaii, and set up the office for Fantasy Geographica on the ground floor of the Ilikai in Honolulu and a secretary in a one-room office, upstairs at the Kona Inn, in Kailua Town on the Big Island. Travis enjoyed Hawaii, but his voice and influence on corporate policy evaporated. Concurrently, Jack lost his input when Emma became ill and he took a six months' leave that stretched to eight. Emma urged Jack to stay with the company for the health insurance, but her melanoma advanced so fast their coverage made little difference.

Jack returned to work at Fantasy Geographica to find himself more of an observer than a participant at meetings. The other founders did not seek his opinions and tended to discount him when he spoke.

The company offered packaged adventures or worked with clients to design special trips. If the clients had the fee, FG would arrange the trip, any trip, like African Safari hunts or thinly veiled "cultural" trips to Thailand. Ping and Buggett became increasingly uncomfortable, outspoken and out-voted. Fantasy Geographica delivered for the client who wanted to "bag an elephant" or the one who wanted to meet a young virgin. And, the 9/11 tragedy ate into these trips, the ones with the largest profit margins.

Linda Lanterman

Chapter 15

Amy realized Harv agonized while she hesitated. His eyes begged her to say *yes*. She turned away. "I, I need to know what the sleeping arrangements will be."

"I, uh, uh I didn't think about it. I mean, well, uh, anything you want."

His lie was so bad, the corners of Amy's lips turned up on their own. She tried to wipe her smile away, but it returned.

"Guess I'm old-fashioned," she said. "I, I understand if you—. Oh, damn you, Harv. You know how I hate it when you assume—. I'm sorry."

"Amy, I love you. I should have told you. I'm just realizing it myself. Do you love me? Could you?"

"Harv, I think I do. Yes, but still—"

*   *   *

Trez waited up for Amy. Two cups of hot chocolate sat on the kitchen table. She'd poured them when Harv's car drove up. She drained the last of hers while she waited for Amy.

"Well?"

"Well, what?"

"No games, girlfriend. Talk to me."

Amy sipped her chocolate. "It's cold."

"Fixed it when you drove up. Zap it a few seconds in the microwave."

"He loves me, Trez. Wants me to go to Hawaii with him. He won a trip to the Big Island." Amy sipped her cold chocolate.

"Hawaii? Nothing about marriage?"

"Trez! This is progress. He never told me he loved me until tonight."

"Okay. That's progress. When? When you going?"

"He suggested a week, or even two, at Christmas, but I'm not sure I'm going."

"Christmas is perfect. Of course you're going."

"Says he thinks he can get two single rooms. Pay the difference."

Trez fixed herself another cup of hot chocolate and stirred it. She didn't say anything. She just watched Amy drink her cold chocolate and stare into space. At last, Trez said, "Ah-uh."

"Trez, I could use some guidance here."

"I need to keep my mouth shut. That's what I think. Don't you go asking Argus, either. This one is all on you, girl."

"Sex will complicate our lives."

Trez patted Amy's hand. "You earned your degree. I have confidence in you. Goodnight now."

Amy could hear Trez humming as she headed to her room.

Chapter 16

It did not surprise Amy that the internship with the City of Oakland was offered at the end of her interview. Treasure Williams seemed to have mystical powers at City Hall. Amy started work the next morning.

A couple weeks later, Amy's papers covered one end of the table in Trez' dining room. Amy began to pick them up when Trez came in from the hospital after midnight and quizzed her about the job at City Hall.

"It's so varied. Never boring. It's easy, yet it's fascinating. In some ways it's more challenging than Cal because I affect people's lives."

Trez looked over her glasses at Amy with an expression that seemed to say *Oh?*

Amy pointed. "Hey, I know where all the restrooms are. I'm asked at least once a day."

Trez wagged her head from one side to the other and gave Amy her *oh, brother* look.

"I develop position papers on renters' rights, property tax exemptions and leash laws."

"What you working on there?"

"It's a kind of feasibility study on a teen curfew."

"That'll never fly."

"Why not?"

"Too many kids have jobs that require odd hours. Emergency situations, and such."

"It's kind of an anti-loitering, anti-drug thing. The whole point is to foster their school work, limit their outside work so they can concentrate on their studies."

"Really? What about the smart young thing who graduates high school at sixteen and works at the hospital to help support her family?"

"She applies to be an emancipated minor."

"Emancipated from what?"

"The law, the curfew, in this case."

"If the law doesn't apply to everyone, maybe we don't need it. We already have anti-loitering and anti-drug laws."

Amy rested her chin on her fist. "You have a point. I better take a close look at those ordinances before I put this together.

"Trez, I've decided I want to go into the non-profit sector. What do you think?"

"Non-profit. Non-profit? Sounds like *poor* to me. Charity. Can a non-profit afford to pay a living wage?"

"Of course, Trez. It's philanthropic work rather than charity. Philanthropy works to correct the root causes of social problems. Charity is direct aid. Both are important." Amy could see by the tolerant look on

Trez's face and knew she wasn't telling her anything she didn't know.

*   *   *

Earlier that same night, in the South Bay Harv tried to get Argus to help him with his problem.

"Well, hello, Dr. Leigh. Where are you? Here in L.A.? What time is it?"

"It's ten-thirty. Sorry to call so late. I'm here in Cupertino. Need some advice, if you don't mind."

"Advice? What could an old garbage man like me have to say to a college professor?"

"You were a vice detective, and you run the Sanitation Department, Argus. It's about Amy."

"Woman trouble. Now you've come to the right man. Hmm. Ah, Harv?"

"Yes."

"You know that I've been a widower for almost seven years?"

"You care about Amy. You know her pretty well."

"Is this about the trip to Hawaii?"

"More than that. Whoa. She tell you about Hawaii?"

"No, son, not a word. Trez spilled the beans."

"I approached the trip all wrong, but I have something bigger in mind. Argus, I'm going to ask her to marry me. Argus?"

After a moment, Harv could hear Argus' deep chuckle as if Argus were in the room with him.

"Congratulations, Harv. Go ahead and ask her. It's obvious to everyone that you two love each other."

"I want it to be perfect. I thought I'd ask her on her birthday, January 25th. You know, plan a romantic evening, dinner, dancing, maybe. Any ideas?"

"Harv, what's the date today?"

"September 16th. Why?"

"Listen to me, son. Trez would not approve of my saying anything, but I'm going to say one thing. That's all. Just one thing."

"What?"

"I know the kind of thinking that goes into this decision. After all that hard work, don't put it off, man. Ask her right away. Oh, it can be romantic, but don't wait."

"But I thought –"

"When do you see her?"

"Next weekend. She's coming down. Thought we'd hike at Rancho San Antonio Saturday."

"Pretty place?"

"Yeah."

"There you go."

"Argus, are you sure? I mean, there's nothing special about this Saturday."

"You're going to make it special, Harv."

"Umm. I'll think about it. I don't have a ring."

"Okay, a second bit of advice. If she says 'yes,' she probably will want some input into the ring."

Argus heard a weak "If?" from Harv but continued. "Tell her what you can spend and shop for it together."

"My God! You're right. I almost blew it. On the ring, you're completely right. She hates it when I make decisions for her.

"Thanks for listening, Argus. I'll think about what you said. I will. I don't know how I'll handle it, but I appreciate your thoughts."

"You're welcome, Dr. Leigh. You do this part right and it'll solve your Hawaii problem. You mark my words. And, don't worry. I won't tell Trez or Amy we talked."

Linda Lanterman

Chapter 17

Amy and Harv sat on a granite outcropping on the crest of the Wildcat Loop trail and watched the oak-forested hills and gold-dry meadows below them. Harv lost himself in the blue warmth of Amy's eyes. He saw love and kindness as he struggled to explain his feelings.

"We have fun together, don't we?"

"Yes, we do. Perfect day. I just hope we don't pick up any ticks."

"Ticks?"

Harv laughed. "The signs warned of rattle snakes, Amy. And you are worried about ticks?"

"Ticks are sneaker than rattlers."

"I want to talk about us."

Amy lifted her ponytail and felt the back of her neck. "Okay. Ticks like to bite the backs of people's necks, you know. What about us?"

"I'm the only one who's going to bite the back of your neck." Harv leaned close. At last he had her full attention. "I love you, Amy. I want to spend my whole life with you."

She searched his face then focused on his mouth. "I love you, Harv."

"Marry me?" He squeezed her hand. He did not anticipate her reaction to his proposal.

"Some day, Harv, yes. Not right away."

Harv wilted. His head dropped. Hurt radiated from his body.

"Harv, Harv. I love you. I've never loved anyone this way." Amy pulled his face up to hers and kissed him. He responded as if he might never see her again.

Gasping for air, he said, "Marry me now. Amy, I love you."

"Harv, it's me. I've worked so hard to prove myself. For some independence."

"Independence? A job? I assumed you would want to work after we were married."

Amy brightened. "Just so it's clear that you're not saving me from my fate, or something."

Harv thought fast. He took both of her hands in his.

"Amy I see us as partners, equal partners, facing life together." If his words surprised him, they also inspired him. "I didn't assume anything, Amy. The reason I don't have a ring today is that I thought we should pick out one together."

Back at Harv's apartment, they phoned Harv's sister in San Diego, Aunt Thora, Argus and Trez. Their emotions began to snowball. They went by the Pings' to pick up Amy's car and her things. The Pings exchanged covert signs of amusement, quick little glances and winks. Apparently, their accommodations were no longer needed. They insisted on taking the young couple to dinner, and they talked about Christmas in Hawaii as a good time for the wedding and a good excuse for them to visit their son, Travis.

"No date yet. Probably a year from now," said Amy.

Everyone else exchanged knowing looks around the table and laughed.

Amy and Harv eventually picked out a brilliant cut, half-carat diamond set in white gold from Gus Mullet & Sons downtown San Jose. The ring and matching wedding band ran over Harv's budget, but he seemed as pleased as Amy was. Their wedding date proved more elusive.

By November, Amy organized her job interview campaign in Santa Clara County. She met with Community Health Initiatives, but found they were volunteer based and not in a position to pay much of a salary. Next, she met with the Committee for School-based Health Clinics at San Jose Hospital, a group even less able to afford paid staff. She talked to the people at Break the Cycle, even though they had no openings. Amy met earnest young community leaders as well as the prosperous and powerful. She talked to interagency groups, for crime and gang prevention, for teen pregnancy prevention and the Interagency Committee for Transportation and Housing.

Amy sat in Trez's dining room studying her Day Planner and tapping the end of her pen on her teeth. "These interviews take some creative scheduling since Oakland City Hall demands a full day's work."

"Stop hitting those teeth. All that money for braces. Now that those wires are gone, you better take care of those teeth." Trez had her hands on her hips, but Amy didn't look up.

"I'm not discouraged, Trez. I'm meeting so many of the players in Santa Clara County. Each interview increases my understanding of the challenges and the possible interventions that people try as they seek solutions."

"Well, you've picked up the lingo. I'll say that."

Amy focused on her mentor. "When you told me to go to some of those interviews to learn from them, to get the big picture, I admit I wondered if it was a waste of time. So Trez, I admit it. You were right."

Trez nodded. "The Community Development Foundation, the interview tomorrow, mention that you've talked to these other agencies. Drop some names. Bring up what you've learned. Show them you have a grasp of the issues, not just the laws."

"You bet."

"Tell them just the way you're telling me. Same enthusiasm, same sincerity. No tooth tapping."

The interview went well. Although the committee could not legally ask Amy about her marriage plans, one member of the panel had admired Amy's ring in the women's room and gathered more information. The fact that Harv was on the DeAnza College staff didn't hurt Amy's chances.

"She's engaged to Dr. Harvey Leigh. He teaches full-time at DeAnza College. They plan to settle here. She wants a career in the private, non-profit sector."

The woman spoke during the panel's ten-minute coffee break between interviews. "I like the idea that everything she's done points her in our direction. She's young. She's bright. She's not someone switching from another career or looking for a position she perceives as easier."

"Or relief from a boring job," said a colleague. "She's got my vote."

Amy didn't convince every panel member so easily. At the end of the day, her name and one other went forward to the Executive Director who had the final determination. Three days later, Amy went to her supervisor in Oakland.

"Zell, I need tomorrow afternoon off for my final interview in San Jose. They just phoned. I know the timing's bad, but they didn't give me any wiggle room." Amy was jumpy, excited but nervous.

"You got it! You're a finalist! Congratulations, girl! Of course, you can have the afternoon off." Zell hugged Amy. "How many finalists?"

"At least two, maybe three. I'm not positive. I'm so nervous."

"Visualize the guy in his underwear, sitting there with a hole in his sock."

Amy laughed. "That's never worked for me. Afraid I'll forget my qualifications or say something stupid."

"Check with Trez. She'll have some pointers for you."

*   *   *

When Amy arrived at her interview she met Fred Greyhound, a crusty, old gentleman who had been on the interview panel. Amy had the feeling he wanted a man in the position.

"Hi, Toots. How ya doin'?"

Toots? Through the open doorway, Amy saw the executive direct look up to watch the exchange with a bemused expression.

"Just fine, Grandpa. Forget your meds?" Amy's eyes danced to her light conversational tone.

Greyhound recoiled into a military salute and smiled without humor. "Touché."

Amy felt heat rising in her cheeks. She hadn't meant to be so caustic. She smiled and held out her hand. "Amy Roth, Mr. Greyhound."

Still at attention and saluting, Greyhound said, "Don't you know how to return a salute, Ms Roth?"

"The Navy doesn't salute uncovered, sir. You must have been Army."

This time Greyhound relented and forced a laugh. He shook Amy's hand then leaned into the Executive Director's office and said, "Well, I couldn't rattle her, Jim. Appears she's had experience with sailors."

*   *   *

"Part of the interview?" Amy's eyebrows arched at the Executive Director. "Pretty creative."

"Oh, Lord, no. That's Fred. He's never going to change." Jim Sparrow came forward to shake her hand and close the door.

Amy wondered if a closed door would keep out Fred Greyhound.

At the end of the interview, the Director said, "You're our strongest candidate, Ms Roth. How soon can you start?"

"January fifteenth."

"Okay. Let's get the paperwork started. I'll make the announcement to the full board Tuesday evening. Can you come down for Tuesday's meeting?"

*　　*　　*

Amy dialed Harv's office before she realized he was in class. She needed to tell someone. She sat in the San Jose parking lot and phoned Trez at Highland Hospital in Oakland.

"The fifteenth?" Trez said.

"Yes. Harv and I talked about extending our Hawaii vacation since I probably won't have any time off until I've worked a year."

"Sounds good to me. Don't you go gettin' married in Hawaii without me. I want to be there."

"I promise, Trez. Can you sneak away for a few minutes tonight? I'll bring you a double latté if you can."

"Have them page me when you get to the hospital, sweet thing. I'll take my break when you get here. Meet in the cafeteria. I'm sure going to miss you."

Linda Lanterman

Chapter 18

At Honokohau Harbor, on the Big Island, Jack Buggett saw a cartoon rabbit on a bulletin board and arranged for *Avenger* to become *Bunny Hop* at the same time he had the white hull painted navy blue. It didn't help. When he tried to discern the color, it still looked red, only darker.

He could not secure a permanent berth, so he sailed the islands, taking temporary berths where he found them. During a stop in Lahaina, he was startled by a familiar voice.

Jack heard Howard Pugh, one of the two remaining founders, call to him from beyond a red haze.

"My God, Jack! It's good to see you. Retirement fits you. New boat? I'm here for a little R and R." Howard winked. "Peg didn't come. Guess you heard 'bout Thurston? It was foul play, of course. Disappeared. No trace. Gotta live life while ya can, I say. You still dive?"

Jack remembered a fiery dawn, rented scuba tanks, his dive flag, red with a white slash, a blood red patch of water under bouncy, pointy waves. He saw red splatters on deck, red smears on his saltwater hose, on his hatchet and fish knife. He squeezed blood from his sponge over the side. He cut and tore away most of Howard's wet suit, then he dreamed he put Howard into 48-gallon red plastic garbage bags. In his mental haze the men he'd killed, Howard Pugh and Thurston James, became a single blurry figure.

Jack returned the tanks to the dive shop in Lahaina and headed across the channel between Maui and Hawaii, back to Honokohau. The sunset lingered into night. Jack began dropping chunks of Howard into the channel. Scraps and tatters of the wet suit followed. He missed a piece.

Howard's left hand and forearm, encased in black insulated rubber, rolled under *Bunny Hop's* dinghy. The arm wedged there until the evening calm gave way to a stiff north wind. Busy with the sails, Jack didn't see the arm tumble overboard.

After midnight, Jack pulled in his sails and came into Honokohau under power. He tied up to the fuel dock and stayed on deck until dawn.

On the Big Island, the Charter Desk had a cancellation. Jack reserved a mooring at the harbor's fuel dock for two and a half months and paid in advance.

*   *   *

Travis Ping flew over to the Big Island and had the former Fantasy Geographica boat, *Lola*, pulled from the stacked storage facility at Honokohau Harbor. She was his now. She spent a day on the ready rack while Travis worked to get her shipshape. The following day he had her lifted into the water, took her out for a quick test run and brought her back to the spot he had reserved on the temporary dock. He was back in time to meet Harv and Amy's flight from the Mainland.

"There he is." Harv waved to a handsome Chinese-Hawaiian man on the far side of the security doors. "The tall, gray-haired man."

Travis had a lei of white and yellow plumeria for Amy and one of maile leaves for Harv.

"Aloha," he said placing the lei over Amy's head and kissing her cheek. Travis kept his eyes on her while Harv made the introductions. Amy blushed.

The two men embraced then shook hands island style, the two-stage grip, thumbs up then fingers clasped. Travis admired Amy's engagement ring and asked about their plans while they waited for the luggage.

"One day for a fast trip around the island. All the rest for fishing." Harv laughed, but Amy knew he wanted to fish as much as possible. The men talked about the boat, *Lola*, as if she were a person.

"Last time I saw *Lola* she was in Honolulu. Lucky for us she's here," said Harv.

"I talked Fantasy Geographica into moving her. Cheaper for the groups to stay in Kona than Honolulu, and you're in blue water right offshore. Don't have to go for miles to get to really deep water."

"Must have been before they cut you loose."

"You got that right." Travis laughed. "She was part of my severance package. Think I told you."

"Sorry. Didn't mean to bring that up."

"Hey, it's fine. As I said on the phone I've taken over Grandpa's insurance business and expanded into boat coverage.

"That reminds me. You still interested in buying her?" Travis looked at Harv, then turned to Amy. "He helped out on several of our Honolulu trips in his college days. Said he wanted to buy *Lola* when he could afford her."

"Great boat," Harv said. "Super little boat."

"Make you a good deal," said Travis.

"You're putting it up for sale here instead of in Honolulu?"

"Yeah, the Kona Coast is the preferred destination for many of the Silicon Valley types. Want to see if I can shake some of those dollars loose."

"She's nice, but I can't afford her," said Harv. And, I understand there's no worse investment than a boat."

"Whatever I get out of it will help. Have my heart on a larger one in Honolulu. If you two catch a record marlin and get your pictures in the paper, mention you caught it on the *Lola*.

"Tell you what, pick up your car, and I'll meet you at the harbor. It's on the way to town. I can talk to Diesel Dan and some of the people there. Don't rush. I have plenty to do."

Amy and Harv rented a red Camaro convertible and headed south on Highway 11. The dry terrain and rocky old lava flows disappointed Amy, although Kona's small international Airport had a certain open-air charm.

"I expected Hawaii to be greener. With palm trees and flowers everywhere."

"Hilo, on the windward side, gets all the rain, usually every day. Orchids grow wild along the roadsides. Look up there, mauka." Harv pointed up slope. "See the green line? That's probably seven hundred to a thousand feet where they get more rain."

"Is that the volcano?"

"That's Hualalai, inactive but not extinct. She's the baby sister of others, Moana Kea and Moana Loa. Kilauea, on the Hilo side is the one erupting. It's been spewing lava into the sea for the last eight or ten years."

"And Moana Loa is the largest mountain in the world if measured from its base on the ocean floor." Amy gave Harv a sideways look and lifted her Plumeria lei up to her nose. "Thought this was your first visit to the Big Island."

"Travis briefed me. Said the lava flows make a stark first impression. I forgot until now. I'll stop lecturing. I promise."

Amy squeezed his hand. "I like Hawaii, lava flows and all.

"Oh yuck!" Amy kicked off her sandal and swatted the mat around her feet, then the car door.

"What's wrong?" Harv swerved, then pulled off onto the shoulder right as Amy smashed a two and a half-inch long cockroach on the dashboard. Yellow roach guts smeared the vinyl. Three detached, claw-like legs swung in the goo. The brown wings splayed out. The antennae continued to twitch.

Harv swallowed hard. "Amy?"

"Hate roaches." She pulled two tissues from her purse and wiped the mess away and cleaned the bottom of her sandal, then rolled the tissues into a ball and dropped it at her feet.

"I've never seen this side of you."

"I can't help it. It's hardwired in my brainstem. The only creature in the world I instinctively kill."

Harv's chin went up then down in a slow nod. "I can live with that. You do realize there are more bugs out here? The warm climate, all the outdoor living. It's only natural."

"Despicable creatures. They spread disease. They survive on almost anything, even paste. Where you see one, there are at least twenty more. They continue to copulate with their heads cut off."

"That, that was more than I needed to know, Amy." Harv swung the car in a U-turn on the two-lane highway and headed back to the airport. "Think we need a different car."

"Yes, good idea," said Amy with a little grin. "I'd never find them all."

*   *   *

In spite of the short distance between the airport and the small boat harbor, it took them an hour to get another car, a dark green Mazda, and find the turn into Gentry's Marina at Honokohau.

"Get lost?" Travis stood at the Harbor House railing with an iced tea and waved. "Come join me."

"Little problem with the car." Harv held up his thumb and forefinger to indicate a three-inch gap. He did not elaborate.

Travis began his crash course instruction about the boat's operation. They finished their tea in the restaurant then went aboard *Lola*. Travis gave Amy and Harv a quick check of the engine, the Magellan Global Positioning System, the autopilot, the emergency gear, and showed them where the charts were stowed and how to make the simple log entries.

Harv took the log. "I never did the log, Travis. What do you include?"

"Date, time out, time on the hour meter, hours fishing, what fish were caught. I note when I buy fuel and how much. Also, any service or repairs and I include any striking observations on the trip, like seeing lots of whales."

Harv thumbed through the log. "Looks straight forward."

"Tomorrow morning we'll take her out for a shakedown cruise. You two can get used to how she handles," said Travis.

They returned to the Harbor House for an early dinner of grilled spearfish sandwiches and chilled schooners of Kona Ale.

Travis took care to include Amy. "*Lola*'s a single screw so you can't maneuver like the larger boats, but it's the same principle as the ski boats Harv said you can handle, Amy, only bigger."

"Her diesel engine's more reliable than gasoline, right, Travis?" Harv glanced at Amy as he asked the question.

"Engine's great. Only time we had a problem was when we had some routine work done and air got into a fuel line. Don't want air in the lines. She's a bitch to start if that happens. Oops. Pardon my language." Travis pursed his lips and looked at Amy. "Anyway, watch your fuel levels. Should check all your fluid levels regularly. Never run a tank out before you switch fuel lines."

Travis tapped his lips. "Trying to think what has changed since you were here, Harv. Oh, I know. New regulations on the way you measure certain species of shoreline fish. They don't use the total length of the fish any more. Measure snout to fork. Use the fork in the tail not the end of the tail. It means minimum sizes have increased. Gives the fish a chance to breed before they're caught."

"Don't have the right gear and why would we fish from shore when we have *Lola*?"

"Pick up the new regs, if you do."

As Harv drove to the harbor the next morning, Amy stared at the sea's explosions along the coast. An unseen storm in the western Pacific spawned the forerunners of a disturbance that promised thunderous crashes through the day and into the night.

"Not too bad," said Harv. "No small craft warnings, yet. Once we're outside the harbor entrance the sea is smooth. Rollers, yes, but the wind is down."

Amy watched the water. "Lot rougher than boat wakes on Lake Coeur d'Alene," she said. "Or even the boat traffic on Isabella. The pounding, the noise. The power."

"Timing is the key," Harv said. "That's what Travis says." The ready dock tilted with the surge. *Lola's* engine rattled loudly and smoked, but within the normal range of a Cummins turbo-diesel.

"Don't worry," said Travis. "We wouldn't go out if it weren't safe."

"I'm not afraid." Amy forced a smile. "With you two guys aboard, I find it scintillating, exciting."

Travis yelled instructions above the noise of the engine adding another element of drama. Harv seemed at ease, so Amy assumed the same attitude.

"Take the helm, Amy," said Travis as they pulled away from the dock in the 5-MPH zone. The snug, small boat harbor at Honokohau greets the sea with two ninety-degree turns, blasted from an old lava flow. Amy over-steered and had trouble staying within the speed limit.

"Her idle speed is a little fast," Harv said. "Pull it in neutral if you need to slow down." Travis or I will take it at the first turn."

Amy nodded and concentrated on the feel of the boat. They proceeded toward the harbor mouth. Harv attached the safety lines to the fishing rods and laid out a selection of lures.

A sea turtle inside the harbor mouth distracted Amy a moment from the waves cresting at the narrow entrance. She turned over the helm when Travis came forward. He timed the set and adjusted the throttle from a rattle to a growl. *Lola* glided up, then down the back of a big roller before it crested.

Travis swung his arm in a northwesterly arc, cupped his hand to his mouth and leaned toward Amy. "Once we reach the Grounds, up there, off the airport near the channel between the Big Island and Maui, the rollers shouldn't present much of a problem."

"Wind's another matter," said Harv under his breath.

A short distance beyond, dolphin surfed the swells near the green marker buoy. Their antics captivated Amy. She wanted to stay and watch them, but *Lola* plowed ahead. The dolphin raced to swim in *Lola's* bow wave and frolicked in her wake.

Travis set the autopilot and joined Harv in easing the lines into the water. Amy marveled at the big, plastic- skirted marlin lures with their stainless steel, Number 8 hooks. She watched the men attach the two longer, heavier lines to the outriggers by running the fishing line up to the top of each one and attaching it to the top of the outrigger with a rubber band. Harv explained that the rubber band snapped and released the line if a fish hit. The men trolled two shorter lines with jet heads in the wake's white water. A boat approached and Harv suggested Amy take the helm. She went forward, pushed the standby button on the autopilot and took the wheel. She knew enough to keep the lines straight. She prayed the other boat would turn away and sighed when it did.

Amy saw the last lure go into the water. She pressed 'auto' on the autopilot and went to the stern for a quick question. "What about the dolphin? Won't they get caught on those?"

"Nah," said Harv. Dolphin never take a lure or a baited hook, although they were known to take the back half of a hooked fish now and then."

"They are too smart," said Travis.

Amy wouldn't have believed it, except she could see the dolphin swimming in Lola's wake and bow wave completely ignoring the lures.

"Amazing! They're like puppies. What fun! The water's so blue, so powerful. My first trip on the ocean."

When the dolphin pod turned back, Amy looked at the mountains. Is that snow?" She pointed to Mauna Kea.

"Sure is. Eleven of the thirteen climatic types are here on the Big Island," said Travis.

Harv rolled his eyes at Amy indicating he thought Travis was overly helpful. She blew Harv a kiss, and he kissed the air back to her.

After a half-hour, the action of the waves felt natural. Amy kept her balance when she pulled a plastic bottle of water from the soft-sided cooler and maneuvered back to her seat at the helm.

"Got your sea legs, I see," Harv said.

Amy enjoyed driving the boat until Harv mentioned how pleased he was she didn't get seasick. Reminiscing, Harv and Travis exchanged all the seasick stories they knew.

"Who was that kid?" Travis scratched his head. "Oh, I remember Roger. Roger Trimble. Poor guy. I can see him on his knees in that back corner of the stern, head hanging over the side, throwing up his whole insides."

"At least he didn't make a mess in the boat." Harv said. "I had to clean up after a couple of kids tossed their cookies. Have to do it fast, before every kid on the boat gets sick too."

"Enough! No more of those stories." The rocking motion of the waves began to get to Amy. Smelly diesel fumes wafted into the boat. She fanned her face with her hand and put *Lola* on autopilot. "Harv, can you take the helm?"

Amy stood and looked at the horizon and back at the land. She breathed deeply. She moved to the portable seat attached on the port side. It was better, but she couldn't completely escape the occasional whiff of diesel. With morbid fascination she watched the rise and fall of the big rollers. From a deep trough, she stared into a wave face higher than *Lola's* canvas top. She wondered how the boat could cling to the surface as it rode up the swell sideways and sank into the next trough. She felt worse. Her skin turned a gray-green. She was close to throwing up and thought death might be okay, compared to how she felt.

"Can we go back now?"

"Pretty soon," said Travis. I've changed our direction so we aren't going with the wind any more. That should help."

Amy considered praying for death, maybe throwing herself overboard. She shot a look at Harv, then at shore. She saw something. A blow.

"What's that?" She knew as soon as she asked. "A whale! A whale! Look!"

Harv and Travis turned in time to see the huge arc of the Humpback with its small, distinctive dorsal fin, curve up and then glide under the water. A second blow signaled another whale, but this one didn't show itself.

"Can we get closer?" Amy snatched her disposable camera, clutched it to her chest and waited for the next sighting.

"Not allowed to approach the whales, Amy. Sorry. However, if they come to check on us, that's another matter." Travis pointed at two more blows farther to starboard than the first two. The whales lifted their flutes into the air and dove.

"That's it. They're headed down," said Travis.

"Look, over there." Harv's voice rang out. "Must be a calf. Look at that little guy! Waving at us. You get a picture, Amy? See the long flipper? The white markings on the underside?"

Amy missed too much action when she tried to align the camera. She gave up on pictures. The rocking boat and the huge expanse of water convinced her she would be better off watching. She wanted to see it all.

"I can't believe how they do that. Like a whole arm out of the water."

"Humpbacks have those distinguishing, long flippers," said Travis. "They migrate through these waters from roughly December through March."

When the whales disappeared, Harv did not go back to seasick stories. "Tell Amy about the carving inside the cabin, Travis."

"Ah, the Eight Immortals. Yes." Travis lifted the hatch cover over the step down into the cuddy cabin and stuck his head inside to look at a small, teak carving of the Eight Immortals in a dragon boat. "They protect the boat and bring good luck at sea."

"Tell her the story," said Harv. "Your uncle."

"It was my uncle's friend. He ordered a nice Taiwan sailboat, built for sailing and chartering in southern California. When it was ready the Taipei boatyard contacted him and asked if he wanted the Eight Immortals. He declined, even though the yard recommended them.

"They shipped the boat and two others to California in cradles on the deck of a freighter. His sailboat was the largest and between the other two. A storm caught the ship, and the sailboat broke loose. Managed to smash both the other boats in the process, and went over the side. The freighter's captain reported it was floating upright, last he saw it.

"Insurance covered most of the loss. When my uncle's friend ordered a new boat, he included the Eight Immortals, first thing."

"So, when Travis bought *Lola* for Fantasy Geographica," Harv said, "he bought that carving for her."

"Makes me feel better," said Amy. "Almost as good as knowing we've turned around."

On the way back to the harbor, the rubber band on the starboard outrigger broke. The Penn 80TW reel screamed. The fish took off for the horizon, running line. Amy handled the boat, no sign of seasickness. Once Harv and Travis had the other lines in and stowed, Travis stood by helping only when needed. Harv fought the fish.

"Marlin! Get the gloves." Harv yelled as the fish began it's leaping fight to dislodge the hooks.

Amy set the autopilot. Travis showed her how to get the gloves for Harv, how to ready the gaff and monitor the autopilot at the same time.

"Keep the line tight. Watch the direction. Use the boat to fight the fish. Pick your times to ready the gear. When there's just two of you, things get busy."

"Damn! He shook it." Harv watched in disbelief. You see it?"

"Amazing!" said Amy. "I've never seen anything fight like that. He stood on his tail. On top of the water!"

"Too bad," said Travis. "Nice striped marlin. I'd say 60 or 70 pounds. Good size for the barbecue. The big blues can be tough. They're better smoked."

After the lines were straightened out and the other gear stowed, Travis turned to Harv, "Nothing like a few whales and hooking a fish to cure queasiness." He quietly indicated Amy with his thumb.

*   *   *

Travis, Harv and Amy fished three of the next four mornings. On Friday they went out in spite of small craft warnings, with afternoon winds predicted out of the north.

"No whitecaps, looks pretty calm. Let's go north, then we can come home with the wind when it comes."

They headed straight out from Honokohau for five miles and then trolled north along the thousand fathom line where an undersea ledge drops away. The sea presented a smooth face, a few rollers but no wind. Off shore from the Natural Energy Lab and the airport, the rubber band broke on the port outrigger, but that was all.

"Want to check the lure? Might have tangled the hooks," said Amy.

"Nah." Harv left the helm. At the stern he watched the 'bird,' a decoy seabird ahead of the leader that implies the presence of baitfish on the surface. Amy took the helm. They stayed at trolling speed, eight to eight and a half knots. Harv cranked the reel a couple of times to double check. "No fish." He turned around with both hands in the air. The same instant the short reel rattled and started spinning, line going out fast. The fish jumped and splashed like crazy.

"Little marlin? Stripy, maybe." Harv said.

"Spearfish," said Travis. "'Bout 25 pounds. Nice fighter. Let's tag this one. For the experience. You can get a tough spearfish once in a while."

Travis showed Amy how to ready the tagging pole and talked her through the process.

"You're lucky to get one good chance. Don't count on a second one. Stand here.

"Try to guide him along this side, Harv."

Harv managed to get the fish along side, but Amy took too long. In spite of Travis' coaching, she made a tentative probe with the sharp tagging stick. She poked at the fish instead of jabbing it. The fish thrashed, shook the hook and swam away without its tag.

When the lines went back into the water and they were underway again, Amy asked, "Do we get a flag?"

"What for? We didn't get the fish," said Travis. "Can't say you tagged it if you didn't."

"I thought fishermen lied a lot."

"They do but not about that. They tend to get imaginative about size and weight."

"Oh," said Amy in a small voice. She liked the idea of fishing flags and wanted to fly one. "What exactly is the purpose of tagging fish?"

"Done properly, tagging lets the fish continue to live and breed." Travis talked while he pulled out the postcard that corresponded to the tag set in their pole. "If someone catches the fish later, the tag provides information that the NOAA (National Oceanic and Atmospheric Administration) scientists use to track migration patterns, growth rates, even speed and distances traveled in some cases. See this," he pointed to the postcard. "You record the time, date, kind of fish, your best guess on the size, weight."

Amy pursed her lips. "Seems like the more they know the more fish will be caught."

"Catch and release programs have caught on with the public," Harv said. "Especially with the big fish that are not that great to eat."

On that note they ate their deli sandwiches. The wind began to lift small whitecaps on the surface farther out.

"That's the wind line," Travis said. "It'll be moving this way before long. We're out pretty far. I think it's best to head home. We can hover along shore if you don't want to go in. The locals call that area close to shore Ono Alley. I'll show you."

Harv wiped his mouth with a paper napkin and yawned. "Sounds fine with me. Maybe a little nap this afternoon." Then he saw it.

A marlin's bill slashed through the water. The marlin toyed with the lure, whacked it, and passed on it. The fish turned. With a whoosh of white water the striped marlin attacked from the side. The reel rattled to life and began screaming. The fish headed away from the boat as fast as he could go.

"He's got it now. Look at that! Slow down. Slow down." Harv yelled over the engine noise.

Amy slowed the engine, pressed the autopilot and rushed to help reel in the other lines.

"Get the short lines, Amy. I'll get the other outrigger."

Harv monitored the fish. Two nearby charter boats circled in the hope of picking up a fish also. Travis kept up his string of commands.

"Get these rods to the forward holders, Harv. Amy, you take the controls." The marlin was still taking line, but more slowly.

"This one's all yours. Act like I'm not here," said Travis.

Yeah, right. Amy switched the autopilot to standby and took the wheel. She hadn't seen the marlin, but she saw the Whitetip. *Lola* was still in calm waters. The windline stayed in the distance, and the calm surface permitted Amy to see to a depth of about twenty feet. The shark didn't break the surface. It stayed with the boat, circling deep.

"We've picked up a shark."

"How big?" Travis looked over the side where Amy pointed. "Ah, small one."

For the first time, the thought of having a gun aboard flickered in Amy's mind. She'd heard that some fishermen do. She rejected the idea, but she no longer was as horrified by it as she once was.

Harv's commands filled the air. "Forward! Forward! Turn! Do you see the line, Amy? Turn! Keep it behind the boat! Gloves! Get the gloves! Too big for us to handle. Set up the tagging gear."

The other lines with their lures and leaders lay coiled on the deck, occasionally tangling Amy's feet as she moved to bring Harv whatever he needed. Travis stayed clear, helping only when necessary.

An hour passed, then another. The shark gave up. "Probably realized he was too small for this particular marlin," said Amy.

An ache developed in her left shoulder. She stood facing the stern and steered the boat with her left hand so she could watch and keep the line in sight.

"Get the fish knife out, hon," Harv called. "Put it on the console, just in case."

The big marlin, a beautiful Blue, swam closer. She was three-quarters the length of the boat. Two hours earlier, Amy missed tagging a spearfish. She determined not to miss again.

Be decisive. Mean it. Only one chance. She leaned over the side with the long pole, tag ready. At last the fish came along side. Amy aimed for the shoulder muscle along side the dorsal fin and plunged in the point. In went the tiny plastic tag. The seven-inch information tube, less than one-third the diameter of a drinking straw trailed along the fin.

Thwack! Immediately the fish reacted. It whacked the side of the boat with its bill. The tail end thrashed violently and drenched Harv and Amy with seawater. The lure fell free.

"There he goes. Angry, but he's alive."

"Thought you said all the big marlin are female, Harv."

"All those five hundred to a thousand pounds or more. Don't know about this one. Not a grander."

Harv inspected the marks the marlin left on the boat. They sat down and drank cold iced tea and caught their breath.

"Great to get the lure back," said Harv.

"Sure is." Travis shook it and checked the skirts and ran his fingers up and down the leader. "You'll need a new leader."

Amy frowned. "What happens if the hooks don't fall out?"

"Have to cut the line, preferably the leader. Save the lure, just loose the hooks. Lure's worth sixty to a hundred dollars. Hate to lose it. A set of stainless hooks runs around twenty-five."

"What about the fish? With those hooks in its mouth?"

"They work their way out. They rattle around, enlarge the hole and fall out, eventually."

A corner of Amy's mouth twitched.

Harv noticed. "That's what they say, Amy. Unless a hook is right in the bill. The bill is very sensitive. All kinds of nerves." Harv thought a moment. "Sometimes a fish doesn't recover, rolls on its side and dies. Either from the fight, trauma to the bill or both. But I've also heard they can survive with a broken bill. Who's to say?"

"About the lure, Harv. Wouldn't it be safer to cut the line? I mean if it didn't fall out by itself? I thought you were going to fall in a couple times."

"No problem."

"It was a problem for me," said Amy. Promise you'll cut the line if there's any danger. I've seen some fishermen without the ends of their fingers. And, I've only been here a few days."

"Don't worry, honey. We won't take chances. That's why we wear these." Harv lifted the fanny pack that held his folded life jacket with its carbon dioxide cylinder. Amy gave him a faint smile. "You're changing the subject."

Harv and Amy studied the Kona Coast charts and satisfied Travis they could handle the boat. Travis flew back to Honolulu a day ahead of schedule. Why not? He carried plenty of insurance, and Harv handled *Lola* almost as well as he did.

Chapter 19

"Let's see if the Nazerovs want to visit the volcano tomorrow," said Harv.

"The couple you knew on the plane? The biology prof and his wife?"

Yes, he specializes in aqua-culture of shrimp and lobster. Kathy teaches history at Berkeley High School. Okay to ask them to go with us? It's ninety miles. Their son lives here. They spend all their free time over here. We can tap into the local fishing lore and learn all kinds of things."

"Nice people," said Amy. "Sure. Kathy said they have a fishing boat, but I haven't see them at the harbor."

"Don't think they'll be going out with the high surf advisory for tomorrow. Let's call them."

Dean drove. Harv rode in front, the women in the back. A red rental car pulled in front of them at the signal at Lako Street as they headed out of town. Amy saw it, but didn't interrupt Dean's fishing story.

Looks like the car we turned in.

At Captain Cook Dean made a quick stop for gas. They followed the only road. Two-lane Highway 19 winds south between Kailua-Kona and Volcano. The Nazerovs told entertaining antidotes about the history of the area. Harv and Amy took in every word. Forty miles farther, it was Harv, however, who solved the riddle of the convertible that stopped in a cloud of dust on a distant rise.

As they approached, four elderly passengers leapt from their car.

"Wonder what's wrong," said Dean.

"Something scared them. Don't think it's engine trouble or a flat," said Kathy. Another car stopped to offer aid. Dean slowed. They all craned their necks as they drove by.

"Something in the car has frightened them," said Dean. "They're terrified. I'll pull off. See if we can help."

"We know that car," said Harv. "Maybe Amy should ride with them."

"Quiet!" Amy pushed Harv's shoulder.

"Cockroaches. You ought to see her. Instant battle mode. A regular berserker. I'd never seen that side of her. She swats them with whatever is handy. She's kind to all the other bugs."

Amy gave Harv another playful punch. Dean stopped the car. The women watched from the backseat. The men walked toward the convertible to see what they could do.

"Your bet's on cockroaches?" Dean smirked.

"It's the look of horror," said Harv as they approached.

"What's the problem?" Dean asked.

"The car's full of roaches. Big ones!" A near-hysterical woman answered. She showed no inclination to get back in the car. Neither did the others.

Harv and Dean looked grave and nodded. "Have a cell phone? You could call the rental company," said Harv.

"We don't have room to take you with us. I suggest you put up with them and return the car," said Dean.

"A huge one crawled up the front of my shirt!" The driver continued to brush away at the front of his shirt.

"You have food in the car?" Harv leaned into the convertible to look. A bakery box from Buns in the Sun lay open on the rear seat.

"That shouldn't matter. We picked this car up yesterday. It's full of roaches! It came that way. I'm not getting in."

"Gets hot out here. Better tough it out and drive back to town. Or, go somewhere so you can wait out of the sun. Ugly, but they don't bite."

"That's not acceptable, young man," said one of the women. I'm calling 911."

Harv and Dean strolled back to their car and reported to Amy and Kathy. "They're talking to the other guy who stopped," said Harv. "Didn't seem interested when I offered them Amy."

*   *   *

At the volcano, the lava flow disappointed Amy until she realized she'd walked for a mile over a flow that was only a few days old. The salt steam and sulfur stink increased the closer they came to the active, open flow. When Amy looked closely, the Earth's red eyes, Pele, Goddess of Fire glared back and made the back of her neck prickle.

"If you don't think the Earth is alive, look there." Amy pointed to the red glow of flowing lava from under the black crust that warmed her tennis shoes and threatened to spill out any moment. The noise of millions of glass shards shattering accompanied every step. Posted notices warned of airborne glass particles and health threats.

"Pele. Capable of great good and great cruelty." Harv put his arm around Amy's shoulders. After twenty minutes, they headed back.

From the demonstration of the Earth's heat and naked power, the couples drove to Puna and Lava Trees National Park in a different climatic zone. Wild orchids lined the road. The moisture floated in air heavy with the scent of flowers and life. Tree boughs arched high overhead to form a leafy tunnel. Impatiens grew wild. Unlike the blacks, browns, sulfur yellows and reds of the volcano, green predominated here. Mist hung in the air. The couples walked the paths of a lush, tropical garden where an old lava flow had surrounded coconut trees, climbed the trunks, and set each ablaze in an embrace of death. When the fires died, the lava cooled in formations standing at different heights, testaments to the living and the dead. Amy found the serenity as powerful as the swirling heat and gases of the volcano.

"God is here," she said. "All the gods are here."

*   *   *

On their return trip, the couples did not reenter Volcano National Park, but ate a late lunch at a café in the town of Volcano, a short way off the highway. They spent some time in the adjoining gallery and quilt shop. They drove back to Kailua Town before dark. They discussed going fishing the next day if there were no high surf warnings.

"Kathy and I like to be on the water by 7 a.m.," said Dean.

Amy and Harv looked at each other with wide eyes. Harv said, "We'll see you out there. We haven't made it before 8:30 or 9 yet."

They all laughed, but Amy turned away, her cheeks ablaze. She swallowed and said, "You get such a different perspective from the water."

"Sure do," said Harv helping her change the subject.

*   *   *

Most mornings Jack Buggett slow-jogged into town from the fuel dock where *Bunny Hop* was moored, then walked back along Highway 11. He swam and snorkeled and fished and made friends with the large Eagle ray that checked the harbor for scraps. He remembered other colors. Back on the Big Island, the red receded until the woman at the charter desk told him they had to move his boat to the pullout dock near the Harbor House restaurant.

"*Amber Rose* needs emergency repairs. She's too big for the other spot. It's a squeeze, but you'll fit. I alerted the boatyard. The guys will help you tie up."

149

"Right away? Today?"

"Today is best. Tomorrow morning would be okay. *Amber Rose* is due tonight, but we could tie her next to you until 8:30. We have seven fishing charters leaving from here tomorrow. Need all the docks. Most of 'em leave at 8:30 or 9 a.m. We'll be jammed if you're still there."

Jack sighed. Red clouds billowed on his mental horizon, but they stayed in the distance, until he saw *Lola*.

*　　*　　*

After Dean and Kathy took them home, Amy and Harv went out for groceries. Downtown, Harv and Amy strolled across the cramped parking lot at KTA Market and through the automatic doors.

Amy looked back. "Did you see the man sitting in the car next to us?"

Harv glanced at the white Mustang convertible. "Can't see him. Top's up. What about him?"

"Sitting there staring into space, zombie-like."

"Maybe his wife's taking too long."

Jack Buggett still sat behind the wheel of his car when Amy and Harv returned with their groceries. He faced forward, a lost, unfocused look on his sunburned, puffy face. Harv did not recognize him, but he had met him only once, many years earlier. Neither Harv nor Amy thought about it until Amy saw the man in the boatyard the next morning, same car, same unblinking, unfocused stare.

Chapter 20

Amy and Harv started early, for them, just after 8 a.m. They found calm seas with four to six foot swells. Amy had the helm while Harv set the outriggers and put the lines in the water. This time he ran the heavy gear short, behind the boat and the lighter gear long, from the outriggers. They went west from Honokohau Harbor for four and a half miles then headed south. Before leaving the dock, Harv made his fishing journal entry and noted that he switched fuel tanks. But writing it and doing it are not the same.

They had a hit. The fish broke the rubber band holding the line to the outrigger and ran twenty feet of line, but missed the hooks. Harv checked the lure and reattached the line to the outrigger. He stood at the helm and watched the sea. Amy finished the morning paper and tucked it away. Every Monday they read Jim Rizzuto's fishing column in *West Hawaii Today*. They had two of Jim's books, including *Fishing Hawaii Offshore*. Harv congratulated himself. Amy's birthday was coming up in January. When he'd noticed Amy thumbing through Shirley Rizzuto's *Fresh Catch of the Day, by the Fishwife*, he bought it, secretly.

Amy moved to the fighting chair, propped her feet on the gunwale and read her paperback. The sound of the diesel engine changed. Amy swung around, looked forward. Harv looked back at her with both hands in the air and a puzzled expression. The engine raced then quit. Before they realized it, *Lola* had sucked her port tank dry.

*   *   *

Amy reminded herself that inboard diesel-powered engines, like *Lola's*, are reliable, more so than gasoline engines. Harv's first reaction was to try to restart it. Perhaps, if they had realized the problem and switched tanks instantly, the engine could have recovered. No doubt they remembered Travis' warning about air in the fuel lines, but neither mentioned it.

Lola swung broadside to the light breeze. She pitched and rolled gently, dead in the water. Amy glanced around, checking for other boats and marking their position with landmarks on shore in Kailua Town. Harv lifted the engine cover and stared in disbelief at the fuel tank valves.

"I meant to change to the starboard tank. Thought I'd changed tanks. I can't understand it. Better bring in the lines."

Amy reeled one of the short lines as he spoke. "I'll get the short ones. If you disconnect the outriggers, I'll get the those, too."

Harv studied the engine, quiet for a while. "Should be able to get it going. We're in a good spot, far enough out."

"Honey, I never touch the tanks without talking to you. You turned on the battery this morning."

"I know. Wrote it in the journal. Thought I'd changed it. Meant to."

Over a mile away, the occupants of another boat noticed them and slowed. "That boat that passed is turning back," said Amy.

"They probably think we have a fish."

Harv pulled out the two-gallon fuel container. "I'll need the tool kit and the large wrench from the bottom drawer in the console."

Amy retrieved the tools. "Want me to hail them?"

"No. Get me a paper towel."

Amy climbed back and forth, opening and closing the engine cover while scrambling to get whatever Harv needed. He worked, butt squeezed on the deck beside the engine. The other boat drew near.

"They're approaching, honey. Want me to hail them?"

"No. I'm not ready for help. Need a couple more paper towels."

Amy gave a friendly wave. No need for alarm. The man at the helm waved back. They didn't stop.

Harv had one of the filters off, a fuel-water separator. "Help me hold this." He poured fuel into the top of the filter and with difficulty, replaced it. "The manual pump doesn't seem to be doing anything."

Amy glanced at shore again and noticed more detail than before.

Diesel ran down Harv's arm to the elbow and onto his shorts. "More towels. Quick!"

The breeze toyed with the water's surface and increased the tempo. *Lola* drifted toward shore at least, not farther out to sea, Australia or Antarctica. Land is scarce between the Big Island and the South Pole. A few boats, white dots, rose and fell on the horizon.

"Should I try the radio?" Amy said, reaching into the radio box. Static answered her. "Channel 68?"

"Honey, 16 is the open channel." Harv's tone said, *not now*. Sweat soaked his shirt.

Amy turned off the radio and stayed quiet. Harv continued to work. "Thirsty. I need something to drink."

"Tea or water?"

He took a couple swigs of Aloha canned iced tea and handed it back. Amy wedged the blue can between the global positioning system and the roll of paper towels, hoping it wouldn't topple with the boat's rocking motion. Harv struggled to his feet. He tried the engine again. Nothing. He glanced around, then returned his attention to the engine. A half-hour passed.

"Want to call someone?" Amy kept her voice neutral.

"Guess we better." Amy didn't mention her thought that the phone might need a charge.

*   *   *

Dean and Kathy Nazerov raced down Palani Road from their house at the thousand-foot elevation. At the harbor they found Mike at the lunch counter.

154

"We need your help."

"Just ordered my lunch. I get half an hour."

Kathy and Dean told him of Harv's emergency phone call. Mike relented. Joel, the woman who runs the marina office, came out as Mike headed in. "The *Lola* just called," she said. "They're in trouble."

"We're going to get her. Soon as we can launch," said Dean.

Dennis, the other boat handler, rushed to clear a path through the busy boatyard. He climbed into the giant forklift, fired it up and hustled to the four-story stacked storage structure. He lifted Dean and Kathy's boat, *Playmate,* from the top level, transferred her to the stationary lift, and then lowered the boat fifteen feet to the water.

*   *   *

Aboard *Lola*, Harv said, "How long you think it will take 'em? Another half hour?" He cast a quick look in the direction of the harbor.

"Only if they fly. More like forty minutes, if they left the instant after we called. Dean said we should tie a white towel to the top of the outrigger." Amy picked up a small white rag.

"Yeah, okay." The white towel was the hand towel Amy used to wipe down the reels after they were hosed with fresh water. She handed it to Harv who tied it to the line and sent it to the top of the outrigger.

Harv pulled out the manual and studied it. He'd done everything, but he tinkered some more. Amy noted boats on the horizon heading back to the harbor. None would approach near enough to hail.

155

Then, in the distance, Amy and Harv saw a boat racing toward the horizon. They thought they could see *Playmate*'s maroon hull. Through the binoculars, Harv verified the dark hull, but the boat continued to move at a forty-five degree angle away from *Lola*. Kathy and Dean didn't see them.

"We don't have their cell phone number."

"Call the house again. Maybe their son is there," said Amy.

Andrei was home and supplied the number. Harv called. As he spoke to Kathy, he detected *Playmate* turn and head their way.

Harv climbed over the windshield and attached a towline to *Lola*'s bow while *Playmate* raced to them.

"Pretty small towel," called Dean when *Playmate* approached within hailing distance. "Your shirt would've been better."

Lola wallowed in *Playmate*'s wake, the tow line taunt. Kathy stood in *Playmate*'s stern, hands to her mouth. "You might as well put out a line."

At *Lola*'s stern, Amy eased a jet head into the water and began releasing line. She kept her thumb on the reel so it wouldn't spin too fast and create a snafu. A mahi-mahi or an ahi would be nice. She relaxed. They were not moving as fast as those fish like, but Kathy was right. Why not put a line out?

Amy felt better while the boats sloshed toward the harbor, but the wind picked up. Around Kaiwi Point, the sea looked like it had an angry rash. If they caught a fish, she knew it would complicate things. She had no idea.

"What was that?" Harv saw a black thing swirl from under *Playmate*'s stern.

"What?" Amy didn't see it.

"Probably a piece of wood or garbage. Better bring in the line. We're getting close."

Amy reached for the reel right as it clicked and spun with its characteristic rattle and ran ten feet of line. "Snagged something. Darn! Not a fish."

She reeled in a black thing. "Snagged something." A chill gripped her. "Harv." Amy's voice sounded different.

"Probably that piece of garbage floating along. Couldn't avoid it." Harv joined Amy in the stern, then he saw it, too.

The second Number 8 stainless steel hook, the gaff hook trailing the silver and blue skirted lure, was buried in the bloated flesh of a human hand.

Harv grabbed the leader and lifted the arm onto the deck. They stared at it. The hook caught in the palm, between third and fourth fingers. No blood. The wetsuit material at the elbow end was ragged. A seam was partially split. The thing looked like a prop for a horror movie.

"Better call the police," said Amy.

"Yeah, the Coast Guard too. Their emergency number is in Honolulu, but they'll get on the horn."

"What about Dean and Kathy? Should we tell them now or wait."

"Tell 'em now, but wait 'til I finish on the phone." Harv dialed the cell phone and looked around for bearings. He went forward and checked the GPS. When he finished, Amy called over the windshield to Kathy. Amy gestured with her hand and a hooking motion. Amy could see Kathy's mouth say *Oh my God! Oh my God!* Without sound. Kathy went to the

157

helm. Dean came to the stern. Harv nodded his head, affirmative, lifted the arm by the leader and held it up a moment. Amy sat with her knuckles pressed to her mouth.

Among the calls Harv made was another one to the marina office. Unflappable Joel listened and answered calmly. "That's a new one. Okay. I'll make some calls. How soon before you get back to the dock?"

*   *   *

The two men who had turned back to check on *Lola* when she first stalled were just forward on the dock from *Lola's* birth.

"I didn't forget you guys," said the man hosing down the boat as Harv tossed *Lola's* line to Dennis. "We're part of US Coast Guard Auxiliary. Call star-USCG for assistance should you ever need help again. We come out for free," the man said. "I still had you in the back of my mind. I wouldn't have forgotten you."

"It's a male thing," said Amy. "He wasn't ready for help when you went by. He thought he could start it. I would have asked you to standby, but…"

"I thought I could get it going," Harv said, shaking his head, still not understanding why the engine had conspired against him. "A bigger problem has come up. Who handles body parts?"

"Body parts?"

Two cops in sharply creased black uniforms and aviator sunglasses came down the steps to the dock. No smiles. The lead cop stepped onto the floating dock and approached with a wide gait.

"You Harvey Leigh?"

Harv nodded.

"Let's see your catch."

The police officers took a few pictures. They dumped the ice from the fifty-pound plastic bag in the fish box and placed the arm in the bag, then packed ice around it. They left the lure attached, simply unhooked the leader, coiled it and placed it in the bag with the arm.

The officers took Harv and Amy's statements and the Nazerovs over lunch at the corner table for six at the Harbor House. The whole place was abuzz with people talking, staring and trying to overhear the questions and answers.

"What an ordeal," Amy said when the policemen left. "I think we owe Dean and Kathy a dinner at Edwards, don't you, Harv?"

"We sure do."

"In addition to lunch here."

"Right."

*   *   *

Harv and Amy stayed at the marina after lunch. Harv got the engine running, but the next morning it refused to start. Diesel Dan checked the engine and diagnosed air still in the lines. Dan listened, checked the engine and showed Harv just where to whack the pump to convince the air to leave.

Linda Lanterman

Chapter 21

"Send Loxie. We could use a good-looking blonde in a tiny bikini." Tim spoke into the phone to the chief agent in Honolulu.

Field rep Tim Tanaka briefed agent Jill "Loxie" Anders over a lunch of ahi poke, local style, and iced tea. Loxie'd arrived on the morning's Aloha flight from Honolulu. She traveled in shorts, on assignment. Tim met her plane and they went directly to the Harbor House at Honokohau. The restaurant is open-air, casual. Sparrows beg, and signs plead with patrons not to feed them. Tim and Loxie talked at a quiet table overlooking the marina. The noon crowd had not filtered in yet. The breeze and the noise of the boatyard covered their conversation. Unnoticed, the sailboat *Bunny Hop* left the dock by the lift and powered silently back to its berth at the fuel dock.

"How come you didn't bring the file?"

Loxie looked up. "Wasn't ready yet. They were waiting for more from California. Said they'd put it on *Tai Pan*. Be here tomorrow."

"Okay, here's what I know. Looks like Buggett's partners used Emma Buggett's death and Jack's grief as an excuse. Some of the employees said Buggett and Ping raised questions and resisted the new direction of the company. Sooo, the transfer to Hawaii plucked one dissident out of the boardroom and the sick wife removed the other one, for a while," said Tim.

"Ping bought the fishing boat, *Lola*, for Fantasy Geographica, eight, ten years ago. The Shamrock."

"Shamrock?"

"That's *Lola's* manufacturer. The factory." Tim extended his hand as if introducing the boat. Down on the water, *Lola* had spot 4 on the temporary dock. Loxie could see the trim white boat with its blue canvas top if she turned around. She didn't bother with another look.

"The company used the boat for snorkel trips, scuba diving, whale watching, fishing," said Tim. "If they need a yacht, the company contracts with a private charter captain. We have the list, the three they use, the *It's Time* here on the Big Island, two on Maui.

"When does our boat get here?"

"*Tai Pan*? Tomorrow, early," said Loxie.

Tim nodded. "Gives us a day to check out the harbor and their place in town.

"So tell me again, why *Lola*'s here and not in Honolulu or Lahiana. This couple? Friends of Ping, right?"

"Yeah, Harvey Leigh and his girlfriend. Leigh has known Ping for years. I'm not clear on all the details, but apparently Ping took the boat in lieu of a severance package, or part of a severance package when the company closed the Honolulu office."

"Smart move after what the company did to Buggett. Maybe he was tipped."

Tim shrugged. "Anyway, as I said, this Harvey Leigh guy knows Ping. Went on several trips Ping led back in the days before the company incorporated. Then, when he was in college, Leigh went on several more summer trips as Ping's assistant. No pay."

"Have enough for a warrant?" Loxie gave him a silly look and waved her chopsticks in the air. "For the Shamrock, I mean? Lot a ways we can do this. Small boat. Wouldn't take long. Simple combination padlock on the cuddy cabin."

"A warrant could be sticky. No direct evidence, and Ping's grandparents still live in Honolulu."

"We're talking Kona, not Honolulu. Maybe the judge won't be so touchy. Who's the judge?"

Tim drew a breath and gave Loxie a flat expression.

"Not Kung?"

Tim nodded. "Yeah, the Honorable Thomas Kung. The one who slapped you Honolulu folks for lack of evidence last year. He'll consider Ping a local boy. We need to do this by the book."

"Ask the Coast Guard if one of us can go along on a routine drug stop. As an observer."

"What if they don't go fishing in the next few days? We could run out of time. The Honolulu lab verified it's Howard Pugh's hand. Someone is killing those Fantasy Geographica guys. Bet Buggett or Veil or Ping is next."

Linda Lanterman

Chapter 22

Amy slipped from the Murphy bed in the living room of their condo and grabbed her cover-up. She paused a moment to look out across Kailua Bay and to marvel at the Pacific. Blue reflected onto the white walls and ceiling of the room. The owners played to the ocean by picking up the deep color with a blue kitchen counter top, pale, gray-blue floor tile, a blue relief map of the island and other details.

Amy and Harv abandoned the bedroom for the Murphy bed so they could enjoy the view, the fresh salt air, and the sounds of crashing waves on the black lava three stories below. In the bedroom the small, high window offered a view of the parking lot, with its odors and sounds of people and cars.

Harv rolled over, opened one eye then both. He took a deep breath and looked at Amy with a hungry smile. "You're up early."

"Time to go fishing."

"We went yesterday."

"I know."

Harv sat up. "Thought I was the one who liked fishing the most."

Out on the water, Harv noticed Amy had her sea legs, the wide stance and flexible knees required for balance in a boat. She scanned the horizon regularly. He thought of Waggles, the Golden Retriever he and Del had as kids. Waggles hunted and pointed birds all on her own, without any training. Harv smiled to himself and focused on Amy. *Definitely has some seafaring genes. No more seasickness.*

"Oh, Harv! Look!" Amy pointed. Harv looked in time to see the explosion of white foam.

"A whole whale! All the way out of the water. It happened so fast."

"Harv?"

"Yes?"

"I think we should retire here."

Harv laughed. He thought a moment. *Retire? That'll be years. Don't say that.* "I'm ready. Marry me when we get home. In the next six months, and we'll retire here when the time comes."

"Okay."

"Really? Wow. Come here."

They kissed until Amy had to come up for air. They missed the Humpback cow and her calf off to starboard. Nor did they see the curious calf's head poke out of the water to check the boat.

*   *   *

Harv had the helm. Amy stood under the canopy facing the stern. She saw the fin. A long bony fin slashed the surface. The older, light reel on the short line let out its distinctive cry the same time Amy did.

"Fish!"

Harv slowed the engine. Amy reeled in the other short line, their teamwork smoother now.

"Mahi-mahi," said Harv. "We eat tonight."

Amy fought the fish. Each time she had it close to the boat, it took off again. She began to tire. It's just a little guy, but he's fighting. Should we release him."

Harv took over. "Eighteen to twenty pounds, I'd say. Hooked with both hooks. Probably kill him to get the hooks out. You saw this morning's paper. They're over-fished every where but here. Hawaii has plenty of 'em, the experts say."

"I think both sides have their experts."

"Think of him as dinner, Amy. Ever had fresh mahi?"

"No."

"You're in for a treat. Get set. Open the fish box. Open the box! Keep the lid ready. I'll grab the leader and swing him into the box. He's going to fight us. Come at us once he's in the box. Be ready."

Amy stood behind the lid she held on end. Harv lifted the small, angry fish into the boat. Jaws working, body thrashing, the mahi-mahi successfully avoided the box. The tail would go in, then spring out.

"The lid! The lid!"

Amy banged the lid down. Before Harv could say, "Stand on it," the fish bounced the lid off and rose on its tail. Harv slammed the lid in place. "Stand on it."

Amy felt the thumping under her feet. The impacts came through the teak and through the thick soles of her Tevas sandals. Amy remembered the surprise in the eye of the predatory ono they caught Monday. Some fish inspire pity, not mahi-mahi.

Harv cleaned up the blood splaters and rinsed the gaff. "Might as well put the lines in on our way back. Where should we get married?"

"Afraid I'll forget my promise? I meant it, Harv." Amy searched through the flags for the one with a blue mahi on a bright yellow background.

"So, where?"

"Mmm, what about Carmel?"

"Perfect!"

"Might be tough to find a place on such short notice, but I'll ask Trez to see what she can do."

"Trez? How would she…"

"She's dying to help with the wedding. We might be sorry if we turn her loose, but I have no doubt she can do it."

They left their mahi to be cleaned and freezer wrapped at the Marina Fish Store. It weighed twenty-one and a half pounds.

Amy and Harv walked across the boatyard just as the Nazerovs brought *Playmate* to the dock flying the orange ono flag. They all stopped at the Harbor House for lunch.

Larry Hite, a charter boat owner, stopped by their table. He traded fish stories and advice.

"Use a wet towel over the head. It disorients the fish. Mahi-mahi calm right down. Then take an ice pick and run it right through the towel into the brain. Customers don't like the bat, too messy. An ice pick is cleaner, faster, and simpler. While the men continued their fish stories, Amy and Kathy switched to wedding plans.

Back at the condo, Amy phoned Trez. It was a long call to the Mainland. Harv read his novel on the lanai and couldn't hear the conversation. Amy came out with her hand on her hip.

"How in the world does Trez know Clint Eastwood?"

"Huh?"

"Well, not personally, but she knows a friend of a friend who knows Clint Eastwood."

Harv waited.

"Apparently, Trez has a whole notebook of plans for us. She was simply waiting for the go-ahead. All that's left for us is the legal stuff, the paperwork. Can you imagine?"

Harv couldn't tell if Amy was pleased or angry. She seemed a little of each. He waited for more clues.

"Another 'friend of a friend' is on the approved caterers list, whatever that is. She has a trio in mind for the music, a retired federal judge to perform the ceremony. Even clippings of wedding dresses. Too much!"

"Doesn't she realize you want to do all that?"

"I told her I wanted Argus to walk down the aisle with me. We agreed on that. But bridesmaids? I wasn't planning on any. Actually, I hadn't thought about bridesmaids at all. Harv, you and I agreed on a small, intimate wedding. Right?"

Harv frowned and scratched his ear.

"Trez knows my financial status. I have a thousand dollars in the bank, but I still owe that much to Aunt Thora for the car."

"Want to elope?"

Amy drew a deep breath. "I like the idea of being a bride. Trez, Auntie, Argus, your sister, they would kill us."

Harv frowned again and tried to look serious. "Didn't you tell me Trez ran her own school board campaigns?"

Amy's head tilted to one side. "A wedding isn't a political campaign."

"She has good organizational skills."

"So do I."

"But you're starting a new job. You will be working that nice fanny off."

Amy started to tap her front teeth with her thumbnail but changed her mind. "So much to think about. We need to keep it light. Not get overly concerned about things."

A serious problem was developing that afternoon, nothing to do with wedding plans.

Chapter 23

Loxie Anders knew she attracted attention. Her job required it. Charter boat captains, hands, the guys who worked the boatyard, middle-aged tourists, all the males, found reason to stand around and gawk. Old guys, wives in tow, pretended to study the boats. The rest made no attempt at subtlety.

"With the temporary dock space right next to them, we can study 'em up close. They won't suspect a thing," said Tim.

Loxie knew better. She understood women had a variety of reactions to her performance, not simple jealousy or embarrassment or contempt. Another woman suspected her faster than a man usually did. It didn't matter. She put on a good show. She didn't mind a bit. The Bureau knew she'd worked the strip clubs off and on during college. She graduated number two in her class from San Jose State University and aced the civil service exam. The FBI varied her locales and assignments. From St. Thomas, Virgin Islands, she'd been assigned to Honolulu, much better than Lincoln or Bayonne or Susanville.

*   *   *

Over their usual lunch at the Harbor House, Loxie and Tim played their roles. Their target couple usually ate at a table closer to the water. Today, friends joined them. Luck placed the two couples where the agents could easily observe them.

"Oh, oh. Ms Roth says you wore the same bikini two days in a row. The guy, Leigh, disagrees." Tim and Loxie kept their voices low, their actions loud.

"Told you. Women pick up on that stuff. I'll go shopping this afternoon."

"She says you scrubbed the deck three times while they ate lunch yesterday. One section four times."

"Oh, geez. Give me a break. All that work for nothing. How'd she know?"

"Must have been watching from here. They can see the boats from where they're seated."

"They listening to her?"

"Not seriously. Laughing. Probably think you're an exhibitionist."

"All that scrubbing for nothing." She picked at a rough edge on a fingernail, then smiled and gave Tim a peck on the cheek.

"Think of it as charity work." Tim said and leaned his head close to hers.

They worked as a team. Loxie kept her face turned to Tim. "Talks with her hands a lot, doesn't she? What are they saying now?"

Tim changed the tilt of his head. Loxie could see he watched the couple from the corner of his eyes, hidden behind dark glasses.

"A concert Saturday at the Mona Lani. Greg can cover it. Roth, she's watching us, you know. I read her lips, but she sees us. Sip your beer."

"I hate the stuff."

Loxie lit a cigarette instead. Her schooner sweat a larger puddle on the weathered plastic laminate table top. She held her cigarette in different poses, but she rarely brought it to her mouth. A waitress brought a coaster and mopped up the puddle.

"I don't think they did it," said Loxie. "Just because they found the arm doesn't mean they murdered the guy. Lots of people would have ignored it. Never mentioned it to the authorities, let alone haul it in."

*   *   *

Thursday, Loxie wore a flesh-toned, string bikini bottom with a spaghetti strapped, see-thorough top that fell above her navel. When Amy and Harv returned from their morning out fishing, they noticed Loxie. Everyone did. She reminded Amy of bare-bottomed toddlers in the Tropics she had seen on television. A couple of fishermen did double takes. A few more wandered over to stand and watch her scrub the sparkling yacht from Honolulu.

"She's collecting a crowd." Amy shook her head and laughed. Harv gave Amy a quick glance and tried not be as obvious as the others.

Loxie looked up when Amy stepped onto the dock. "Any fish today?"

"Nah. We'd have a flag up if we caught one," said Amy. "We had a hit. Tore up the lure but didn't get hooked. Probably an ono." Amy showed the slashed lure, a silver-skirted jet head, to Loxie.

"Not a marlin?"

"Marlin tend to beat up the leader, take nicks out of it. But we didn't see the fish."

"Well, good luck tomorrow."

"Thanks."

"You go out every day?"

"Almost."

"Guess I'll see you tomorrow, then."

"Maybe."

*   *   *

Tim observed Harv mopping the deck through the yacht's small smoked glass portholes. Loxie popped inside. Tim came into the main cabin. "They going out tomorrow?"

"She didn't say for sure. You notice anything?"

"Nope."

"I really don't think they did it, but my tan's coming along." Loxie checked her reflection in the cabin mirror and went back out on deck.

Chapter 24

"How in the hell did you lose the boat?"

Tim pulled the phone away from his ear and winced. Loxie heard the angry words across *Tai Pan's* main cabin.

"We were gone less than half an hour. For take-out. Loxie needed a new swimsuit. The Roth woman mentioned seeing her in the same one. Thought we could save time. Thought we better—"

Loxie frowned. She bought her new suit in less than ten minutes, hadn't even bothered to try it on, but it didn't matter. They'd violated procedure. One of them should have stayed with the boat at all times. Trouble was, the *Lola* vanished while they were gone. She was glad Tim took the call. The boss was hot.

"Yes, sir. We will, sir." Tim did lots of nodding. "Leigh and his girlfriend are at their Sea Village condo. Don't know it's gone."

*   *   *

Harv and Amy took an ice tea break on their lanai in the late afternoon and watched a pod of Spinner dolphin play two hundred yards offshore. When the phone rang, Amy assumed it was Trez with more wedding ideas. Amy heard the urgency in the tone, before she registered whose voice it was. The woman calling from the marina didn't sound like herself either.

"Amy? Did Harv take the boat out?"

"Joel? What is it? Harv's here. Want to talk to him?" Harv turned to watch Amy.

"You guys having work done on your boat? Someone doing a test run?"

Amy heard her own voice change. It became lower, deadly serious. "Our boat's gone, Joel?" Harv was on his feet, close to Amy.

"We have three guys working today. Dennis just brought it to my attention. He's in here now. I guess Harv told him you weren't going out until tomorrow. That's why he's suspicious. Your boat's gone."

"Did anyone see anything. A mechanic? Anyone on the boat?"

"No one I've talked to. I'll call the Coast Guard, just wanted to check with you first to verify you weren't using it. You are sure no one was going to do any work on it?"

"Positive. Here's Harv."

"It's only been about two and half, maybe three hours since we were there. Can any of the guys pinpoint seeing the boat after we left?"

"It's been busy, Harv. Several boats needed to be moved from stacked storage for repairs. They've been in the back of the yard mostly. Dennis noticed your boat was gone and checked around. No one he's talked to saw anyone near your boat.

"I need to call the Coast Guard right away. They can't go far. Did you leave the key on board?"

"Locked in the cuddy cabin with the fishing gear. A combination padlock. Could be pried right off.

On their way back to Honokohau Harbor, Harv said, "Why steal a boat? People everywhere will be looking for it. What's the point? Every harbor will be notified. Coast Guard. People at fuel docks. Harbor masters—"

Amy realized she had not seen the Coast Guard around lately, but she kept quiet. Members of the Coast Guard Auxiliary were there, of course. Somewhere.

"Not our boat. Travis' boat. Not our boat. Who would steal an ordinary fishing boat? It's not fast or fancy. How am I going to tell Travis?" Harv drove the six miles to the harbor repeating his questions, talking to the steering wheel.

Amy thought of the diesel smell and the smoky exhaust fumes, but she wondered aloud about the registration papers.

"In the boat," said Harv.

"It's a great little boat, darling. We'll get it back."

At 3:40 p.m., Harv and Amy tore into the work area at the marina. Harv dodged a Zodiac on its trailer as a man tried to maneuver it into a parking place after its afternoon snorkel trip to Kealakekua Bay. Harv parked at the harbor office. In the adjoining parking space, a man sat in his seatbelt behind the wheel of a rusty, white Toyota pick-up. He had red-rimmed, double-pouched eyes. When he glanced at the couple, he betrayed no expression. His face was flat.

Inside the office, Harv said, "That the same guy whose wife was taking too long in the market? Different car."

"I don't know. Could be." Amy looked at Harv with a half smile and a little frown. "He looks desperate. Keeps checking his rearview mirror."

From the marina office, Amy and Harv rushed to the Hawaii Department of Land and Natural Resources, Boating and Ocean Recreation Division in another building, adjoining the front parking lot. The office closed at four. The man behind the counter took a formal report and sympathized. Harv asked about what would happen next.

"First, we fill out this Incident Report. You said the owner will be here Monday? We need to talk to him. Next, we conduct an investigation. To be honest, sir, chances of recovery are not good. Thousands of small boats get stolen every year. Lots of isolated coves. We don't have the manpower to search for stolen boats."

Harv's face fell.

"We send the report to all harbors. They post it. We notify the Coast Guard."

"Coast Guard has the report," said Harv.

"And," the man behind the counter pulled out a binder, "since it could fit on a trailer, if someone had a big enough one, that's another problem. They could take the boat inland, paint it, change the numbers, rig it differently."

"But if we could let everyone know today, our chances would be better. Before any changes get made.

Before it gets far." The outside edge of Harv's hands bounced up and down on the counter, pleading.

Across the counter, the man flipped through the stolen boat notices, silently showing Harv his was not the only one. "Most of these are from Oahu. Haven't had a boat taken here for eleven, twelve months."

"Can't anyone check around today?"

"We'll post it, sir. Do you have a picture we can use? Pictures help."

"Yeah, okay. I'll get some." Harv let Amy lead him outside. "I need to call Travis."

In Honolulu, Travis listened, then said, "This afternoon? In broad daylight? Gutsy. Well, it's insured, Harv. Don't take it so badly. Chances are they'll find it in the next few days. Kona's not that big. Someone will see something sooner or later. I can't get there until Monday. No one in the office until then anyway."

"We fly home Sunday."

"Don't worry. You guys didn't witness anything. You've made your report. That's all you can do. Any other developments on the arm you found?"

"You know what we know. Lots of speculation on television news out of Honolulu. Lost a couple divers here this month, and there's a missing person's report from Maui. Guess they're running tests."

Linda Lanterman

Chapter 25

The cops in Kailua-Kona are stretched pretty thin. Bob Kokuakane took the stolen vehicle report from his cousin's uncle even though he was off-duty. It provided a chance for his boys to fish at Keahou Bay at sunset. His cousin's uncle left the keys in his rusty, white Toyota pick-up. He returned from fishing, moored his Alii Kai boat in the narrow bay and discovered he had no way home.

Kokuakane knew the little truck. "Crime of opportunity, Uncle. Can't leave your keys in the ignition. Some keiki comes along and decides to take a ride."

"Hey, Dad. Got one!"

Kokuakane turned. He waved to his kids, then he saw the boat. It wasn't one of the usual boats at Keahou, but he remembered it. "That boat. You know that boat, Uncle?"

"No. Some haole's, I bet ya. Leave his boat here couple days. Never saw it before that."

"I have. Keep an eye on the boys, will you? I need to call the station."

181

*　　　*　　　*

"Officer Kokuakane is on the scene. Keys are in it. Can you get to Keahou Bay right away?"

"Sure." Harv turned to Amy. "They found the boat."

"We'd like you to take the boat back to Honokohau, Dr. Leigh. More security there."

"That's where it was stolen."

"The marina has a night watchman. The Division of Land and Natural Resources is there. We think it would be safer, but it's up to you. The fingerprint guy is almost done."

*　　　*　　　*

The combination lock lay on the deck. The rods and reels were not as Harv and Amy left them, but they were there.

"I can't believe it. Looks like a broken lock, some scratches, dents. Nothing's missing that I can tell," said Harv.

"They took down the carving of the Eight Immortals," said Amy. She checked the cuddy cabin with the flashlight. "How odd. Took it down, but left it." She crawled over the stored gear and retrieved the carving. She turned it in her hand and saw the long groove in the underside of the dragon boat. "Suppose something was hidden in here?"

*　　　*　　　*

182

On their last night in town Harv and Amy went out to dinner at one of Kailua's excellent oceanfront restaurants. Harv ordered Mac nut encrusted opakapaka, Amy the grilled mahi-mahi with mango salsa. They had a table by the surf. Amy noticed movement. A large roach wondered in from the seaside and investigated the low lava rock wall. Amy followed the creature's progress along the top of the wall and down to the floor of the lanai.

"What are you watching?"

"An uninvited guest."

The roach emerged onto the tiled lanai and started for their table. A man at the next table saw it too. He put his finger to his lips and gave a slight nod at his wife.

"Where is it now?" Harv casually looked around for the first time.

"Coming toward my foot," said Amy, sipping her wine, eyes alert.

"I suppose you're going to kill it?"

Amy tapped the roach hard with her foot. Harv heard a *crunch*, but not a *squish*. Amy killed the bug without smashing it.

"Now what?" Harv wanted to know. He didn't appear to fully appreciate of Amy's restraint.

Amy flicked the toe of her sandal and the roach slid across the floor back to the lava wall. "Ants will clean it up," she said.

Dinner was excellent.

*　　　*　　　*

Amy and Harv returned to California Sunday, as planned. Travis Ping flew to Kona on Monday. He signed some forms for the Boating and Recreation Division, then arranged for a high-pressure wash of *Lola's* hull and some touchup work on the paint. He signed more papers in the yacht broker's office and flew back to Honolulu the same day. *Lola* was for sale.

Chapter 26

"Orange? Orange, Trez?"

"Not or-ange, Sunset orange. I sent samples to Thora and Del. Did you know orange is your aunt's favorite color?"

"Trez, that's not a recommendation. Why orange?"

"Didn't send you a fabric sample 'cuz I have the files ready for you. You can go through everything at once. The trio has a gig at the restaurant. Jack London Square. You know how to get there, right?"

"Yes. Trez?" Amy drew a breath. "Oh, nothing."

"It's going to be beautiful, Amy."

"Yes, Trez."

"How's work?"

"Busy, but fun. I have the regular workday, then all these outside events to cover. More hours than I figured. I'm enjoying it, though.

"Orange, Trez?"

"Don't obsess, little sister. Wait until you see the whole picture."

185

"Okay, Trez. See you Sunday." Amy hung up the phone. Harv looked up and waited.

"Wedding party's wearing orange." Amy's hands flared out. Mirth twitched across her face.

"Me too?"

"No, a black tux for you and the men. You get a sunset boutonniere, an orange rose bud. Auntie Thora and your sister already have plans to coordinate their dresses in a deeper shade of orange. Your sister? And, I'd like to know, how in the world does Trez know Clint Eastwood? I forgot to ask."

Harv busied himself with various expressions he hoped conveyed sympathetic understanding, but amusement twinkled in his eyes and played across his face. "Eastwood used to be mayor of Carmel. Does he still own the Hog's Breath?"

"Well, not personally. She never said she'd met him. Trez knows a friend of a friend who belongs to Tehama Golf Club in Carmel. This same 'friend of a friend' also knows someone on the approved caterers list. She says the guys in the trio can double as ushers."

Harv noticed they were talking past each other. Amy addressed the floor, the ceiling, the front door, but she wasn't angry. At last, she focused on him.

"You okay with all of this, honey? I keep telling myself that nothing is going to spoil our day. Nothing. I won't let anything upset you or me or our day, and it's going to be a wonderful day we'll always remember."

*   *   *

Amy's discreet inquiries confirmed that Eastwood's Tehama Golf Club was so exclusive that it could not be found on maps. She didn't find anyone who had been there. A couple people told her what they heard from others. Of course, it was new, but one source told her the 25000 Via Mulpaso address in Carmel Valley yielded a guard in his car on the side of a road no bigger than a driveway and a white board fence that might lead to another horse pasture. No sign, no numbers. After about three and a half miles on the winding lane, it ended on a hilltop that forced Californians to realize the Coast Range were mountains and not "hills." The panorama provided an amazing view of undeveloped hills and Monterey Bay in the distance. Valets drove all cars immediately away to invisible underground parking.

The snatches of information intrigued Amy. She wondered if Trez had pictures.

*　　　*　　　*

Traffic delayed Harv and Amy about twenty minutes so when they arrived at Oakland's Jack London Square, Harv dropped Amy at the restaurant and went to find parking.

"So, so good to see you, Trez," said Amy when the two embraced at the table. She felt her concerns about the wedding melt away. "Harv's parking. Said to start without him."

"Before I forget, this came for you." Trez handed Amy an official, legal-sized envelope from the Seattle Superior Court. "Looks like a jury summons, except it's from Seattle."

"What on earth?" Amy read the page twice.

Trez watched a series of emotions grip Amy. First came the widening eyes and firmer grip of her fingers on the page, then the pause of recognition. Next came the narrowing of the eyes, not hatred exactly, but close to it. Trez saw Amy's features return to normal. One corner of her mouth moved. Amy read it twice. She checked the back of the form, nothing. It was a form of some kind, a full page of text. Trez bit her tongue, then cleared her throat.

Amy sailed the sheet at Trez. "A sentencing report for one Rick Horner. The creep on the plane. Sat next to me from Spokane to Seattle. I told you."

Trez skimmed the page. Amy picked up the envelope. "How in the world?"

"Argus," said Trez.

"Of course."

"He'll deny it, but he must have asked someone to track the man for him. Says here Mr. Horner gets eight to ten years for the attempted murder of Jackie 'Brandy' Snodepen."

Harv found Amy and Trez pouring over wedding gown pictures and sketches and drinking red wine.

"We ordered a bottle," said Amy with a giggle. "Celebrating."

"I see." Harv glanced at the musicians, a jazz trio, piano, bass, and drums. "Great music."

"There you go. Another decision made," said Trez. "Did you bring your checkbook? We can nail them down tonight."

Harv thought the evening was going well until after dinner when he returned from the restroom. He heard Amy's stern voice.

"No, Trez. No way. She's a great dog, but Quito's not going to be in the wedding. I mean it, Trez."

"Well, I haven't checked. They might not allow dogs anyway. I planned to call tomorrow."

Harv jumped into the fray. "Trez. We don't want Quito upstaging the bride."

Amy gave him a sharp look, then laughed and said, "Thanks, Harv."

"I mean a dog's distracting. Quito's presence would be so unusual. Someone would have to mind her. Pick up after her."

"Okay, bad idea," said Trez.

She crossed off a line in her notes and continued. "We decided on Mai as the bridesmaid and me as Matron of Honor."

"Mai's my closest friend from Cal. If I ask anyone else, it would be really hard to limit the number," said Amy. Harv listened with one ear. He watched the musicians and kept time with the beat.

"The rehearsal will be brief and right before the real thing," said Trez. "We run through it before the other guests arrive, with or without the bride. How old-fashioned are you, Amy? Okay to see Harv before the ceremony?"

On the drive back to Sunnyvale, Amy said, "Pretty clever. Pretty clever."

"What?"

"I finally figured out Trez' BATNA."

"BATNA?"

"Best alternative to a negotiated settlement. That business about Quito was a throwaway to make her look reasonable. She didn't fight us on that because she never intended to."

"She didn't fight us on anything, Hon. It all sounded perfectly agreeable to me. I get the girl."

*   *   *

The Kona police found the stolen Toyota pick-up in the marina parking lot nine hours after it was reported missing, but it was the FBI, Tim Tanaka and Loxie Anders, who eventually put all the pieces together. As soon as they realized Jack Buggett's boat, repainted and renamed, was at Honokohau, right under their noses, they arrested Jack.

The charges included suspicion of murder in Howard Pugh's death, a suspect in Thurston James' disappearance and an obscure charge, later dropped, about stealing China's national treasures. Among the items in Jack's possession, aboard *Bunny Hop*, were three jade pieces, identical in size and shape, but with varying patterns of tiny holes.

*   *   *

Jack babbled about the Eight Immortals and the dragon boat. "No, I didn't steal the boat. Left it tied to the dock, inside the cuddy cabin."

"Mr. Buggett, tell me about this." Loxie took her turn at Jack. She held one of the jade pieces in her palm so he could see it.

190

"Emma liked the ring." Jack looked up with innocent, weary eyes. "She opened the red brocade box. Cried when she saw it." His face took on a glow. "You like it, don't you, Emma. You didn't die. It protected you. Emma, don't die."

In his call to the Honolulu office, Tim said, "Yeah, he's being cooperative, talking, but there's a screw loose. We'll need a full psychological evaluation."

Loxie overheard the conversation and nodded her agreement.

Tim listened, then said, "No, I don't think so. I think we have a genuine nut. Loxie'll bring him over tomorrow. She wants our folks to get a warrant for his house on the Mainland, in Sunnyvale. Go through every inch. In addition to all the usual stuff, let us know if they find a red brocade jewelry box. A small ring box, red borcade."

"Check any safe deposit boxes, too," said Loxie.

When Tim finished, Loxie said, "I think we might have a strong case for asset seizure here. Sure would like to keep that sailboat."

Loxie, no longer in her bikini, but in black slacks and a lightweight black jacket, accompanied Jack off island to face a federal magistrate in Honolulu. Tim secured *Bunny Hop*.

Jack was often incoherent, but Honolulu forensics had fresh fingerprints, lifted from the *Lola*, that matched Jack's. Harbor receipts placed him in Lahaina when Howard Pugh disappeared. An employee of the dive shop where the men rented their tanks identified Pugh and Buggett from photographs.

Armed with a warrant and in spite of the efforts to clean his Sunnyvale home, agents found some hairs and blood stains in the garage that matched Thurston James.

The Honolulu FBI agents had long sessions with Travis Ping. They wanted to know all about the time Jack spent in Honolulu, before Fantasy Geographica laid off the two of them.

"Tell us again why Buggett suspected the container?"

"I don't know why he suspected it, other than the bill of lading, as I told you. That particular shipment didn't require a whole container, in Jack's opinion.

"His father had been in the Quartermaster Corps," Travis said. "Jack was our best man on inventory control. He said we should check it. The US Customs officer came with us. He can tell you we were the ones who thought something was amiss. We opened the container and started matching numbers. Didn't have to go far. About a third of the stuff was ours. Fantasy Geographica paid for the whole shipment but most of it wasn't ours. Vases, terra cotta figurines, ancient pieces. I went with the Customs man to phone his boss. Jack stayed with the container.

"I didn't see anything small. The crates were all large, carefully packed. We opened two."

"Care to speculate?"

"Probably shouldn't. All I can guess is that Jack might have found something in one of the crates we opened. We pulled out a couple bundles, unwrapped them. Realized they were definitely not what we ordered and went for backup."

"I don't understand it," said Travis. "Jack always did the right thing. I'll never forget the time some kids pressed him on marijuana. The usual, on how it wasn't any more dangerous than alcohol. They knew their facts. Jack didn't preach or lie. He said, 'I admit I use alcohol. Marijuana doesn't tempt me. I don't need any more bad habits.' It was the best thing he could have said. It was honest. He gave those kids a quick comeback, something they could use against peer pressure.

"Maybe he was under too much stress and he had a breakdown."

Linda Lanterman

Chapter 27

The day before the wedding Amy rode to Monterey with Trez, Aunt Thora and Helen, Argus' new lady friend. With their gowns and luggage, they squeezed into Trez' 1990 Cadillac Coupe de Ville, newly repainted a deep forest green. They chatted the whole way, scarcely noticing the traffic. Mai Ip, Amy's friend from Cal drove separately in Amy's car. It was Amy's car, free and clear, a wedding gift from Aunt Thora.

Harv planned to rent a Chevy Caprice, but Travis and Argus vetoed the idea at the Hertz counter.

"It's your wedding, Harv. Drive something that fits the occasion," said Travis.

"I am not squeezing my sorry ass in the back of a Chevy, son," said Argus with a tone and a glare that made Harv wonder whether he was kidding or not. Harv let them talk him into something fancier. They drove to Carmel in a Lexus LS400. Travis, Harv's best man, rode shotgun and Argus stretched out in the back seat.

The trio plus two, a trumpet and an alto sax player, traveled in four cars. Part of their

195

compensation, negotiated by Trez, was a night's lodging and dinner at the Sheep Ranch. The piano player relieved the musician at the restaurant for a jazz set. The other members of the group had to pull him away when it was time to go.

Amy awoke Sunday morning and dressed for a jog on the beach.

"Amy? What time is it?" Auntie Thora spoke into the darkened room they shared.

"It's 6:20. Didn't mean to wake you. Sorry."

"What are you doing up?"

"Going for a run. Want me to bring you a scone from The Tuck Box? They are famous for their homemade preserves and scones."

"No need. They have a continental breakfast here. Just don't come back too early. Take your key."

"Got it." Amy patted her pocket and was out the door.

From the beach, she headed for Ocean Avenue, Carmel's main street that runs from Highway 1 to the water. She breathed in the cool, salty air, and crushed pine needles in her hand and sniffed. Sunlight sparkled on the waves. She passed a house with hundreds of little pink begonias in bloom, another had a mass of marguerites, a third had miniature marigolds along a winding stone path to the front door. She absorbed the storybook character of the pre-World War II homes on their tiny lots. The huge Monterey Pines and lush flower gardens enchanted her. The town made her feel the way she imagined Europe or a place in a fairy tale. Many of the shops and galleries were intimate. Most of the restaurants were elegantly small, with inner courtyards. The wedding party ate dinner that evening at Little Napoli, renown for their family recipes. Amy resolved that she and Harv would visit Carmel often.

*   *   *

"Only a half hour late. Not bad." At the wheel, Trez stuck out her chin and smiled. Amy and her attendants headed for Tehama.

She was calm. "You built extra time into your schedule, didn't you, Trez?"

Trez gave her a quick look in reply. In Carmel Valley, they found Via Mulpaso and the unimposing white fence. They answered the guard's questions and he permitted them to pass. Trez drove along the bottom of a snug, oak-shaded valley.

"Gee this is narrow," said Amy. "I can't see the sky. Can you, Trez?"

"Only in snatches, but I need to watch the road. Don't want to go in the ditch."

The steep hillsides wore the velvet green of spring, but when the road climbed, green transitioned to tawny brown, or gold, as Californians call it. Green grass on the hilltops hung on only under the scattering of massive live oaks.

"Oh, look!" Amy said. "There, on the horizon. That's Monterey Bay sparkling in the distance."

"I'm more concerned with the sky," said Trez. "We don't want any clouds or fog today."

"None in sight," Auntie Thora sang out from the back seat where she couldn't possibly see much of the sky.

Amy kept her eyes on the beautiful expanse before her. She experienced an epiphany that made her a Californian, but she kept her lighthearted thought to herself.

Of course blue and gold are Cal's colors. How silly of Stanford to choose red.

"Look how the restive sea kisses the delicate sky," said Aunt Thora.

Amy and Trez exchanged glances. "Ahh, romance," said Trez. "It's rubbing off on all of us."

*   *   *

The classic Hacienda style of Tehama incorporates traditions of the Moors, Southern Spain, Mexico and early California. Amy delighted in the sunny, inner courtyard with its paving tiles and large fountain. Inside the main banquet room, with its huge fireplaces in each corner at the far end, Tehama's Events Coordinator stood taller when Amy exclaimed about the room's magnificence.

"As you can see, we have hammered wrought iron work and heavy timbers over steel construction. The Carmel Stone walls are dry laid," he said. "The mortar is halfway back, not flush with the stone, to offer the dark line you see. Very pleasing to the eye." Amy fingered the rough texture of the stone, turned and smiled up at the high ceiling with its chandeliers.

Perhaps mindful of the wedding, the Events Coordinator added, "Beautiful as they are now, at night those faux alabaster chandeliers bathe the room with warmth and romance."

Amy's one moment of misgiving hit hard. It came when she first saw her bridesmaid, Mai and Trez, her Matron of Honor, come into the room where she was dressing. Amy's lips folded in, over her teeth.

"You okay? You look sick." Trez said. "Not getting jittery, are you?"

Amy looked at her bridesmaid and her Matron of Honor, in their shimmering orange silk taffeta. In a small voice she said, "No, I'm fine. Just fine."

She quickly turned away. *Oh, my God. That's a lot of orange. Trez, you witch, you only showed me a tiny swatch of fabric.*

"Ta-da!" Aunt Thora burst into the room and struck a model's pose. She wore a deeper, more subdued orange.

"Oh, Auntie, you look fabulous. That color looks great on you."

"You like it? Not too bright?"

"No, it's great. You should wear it more often."

"I've always liked it, but didn't know how it would go over in Bakersfield."

"Shake them up a little, Auntie."

"Yes." Thora appraised her reflection in a huge, gilt-framed mirror. "I may never take it off. Think I'll sleep in it tonight."

*　　*　　*

Amy peeked out at the Terrace when the time drew near. Everyone she could see wore sunglasses. The usher/musicians seated the last of the guests. They sat facing west into the setting sun, a place of honor in Nature's cathedral. Scattered clouds sculpted the sky.

"After my sweet, departed wife, you're the most beautiful bride I ever saw." Argus squeezed her arm. "Stay calm now."

"I am. Must be bright out there. Wonder if Trez wants us to wear sunglasses?"

Argus rolled his eyes. "Don't be silly. Where is she anyway?"

"Right here." Trez took her place in line behind Amy's friend Mai who was listening for her musical cue. "Needed to thank the Lord for this perfect day. No fog."

"Trez," said Amy. "You arranged the perfect wedding. Thank you."

The "thank you" was said to Trez' back as she stepped outside after Mai and started down the aisle. The trumpet player provided the music. Purcell's *Trumpet Solitaire* summoned the angels, crossed the hilltops, floated down the canyons and rode air currents to the bay. Hankies and tissues fluttered.

"Ready?" Argus gave Amy a quick look. They started down the aisle.

Amy's mouth opened. "Look."

"I'll be damned."

"How'd she know?"

The whole sky was orange. Fire-orange flared where the sun dipped behind a hill, then the sky shimmered into the exact color of the attendants' dresses. Argus patted Amy's arm. He wore a proud smile. His eyes watered.

*   *   *

"So Trez got you out on the dance floor, Travis. Some dancing." Harv pulled out a chair for his Best Man and handed him a linen napkin to mop the sweat from his face.

"You see that old woman dance? She's something." Travis shook his head and laughed.

"Who you calling old? I notice you tired pretty quick," said Trez. "We'll have another go after you rest, old man." Trez spied another victim and headed for him.

Amy and Harv paused to sit with Travis for a moment. They'd completed their round of greetings and danced their first few dances. Soon they would cut the cake.

Aunt Thora saw Trez cross her fingers when the cake-cutting announcement was made. Across the table she saw Argus press his lips together and shoot Trez a look.

"What is it?" Thora asked.

Trez looked at Thora. "Nothing, really."

"It's the test. The test of a lasting marriage," said Argus.

"It's superstition. That's all. Silly." Trez shrugged, but Aunt Thora's eyes bored into Argus.

"If either the bride or groom smears cake on the other it's a bad sign," said Argus.

"Well, it certainly is," said Aunt Thora. "I'm sure that won't happen tonight."

Under the table, behind the tablecloth, Thora crossed her fingers. Bride and groom completed the cake-cutting ceremony without any mess. No one paid attention to the extra champagne toast among Argus, Trez, Thora and the others at their table.

Amy and Harv had an abbreviated, one-night honeymoon at Highlands Inn. They planned to have a real, Kona honeymoon, in June after school was out for Harv and things slowed a bit for Amy.

Chapter 28

"Jill Anders."

"Loxie?"

"Is this Amy Roth?"

"Yes, Amy Leigh now. I married Harv. We talked to you in Kona. The Fantasy Geographica murders."

"I remember. What can I do for you, Mrs. Leigh?"

"It's about the jade pieces."

"Evidence. Property of the People's Republic of China. After the trial they will be returned."

"Hear me out, please. China doesn't know about them."

"Ms Roth—"

"Please. Listen to me."

Loxie listened. It was impossible, of course. She said so. She promised nothing, only to call Amy back some time later, but Amy's suggestion pushed into Loxie's thoughts at odd moments and interrupted her work. She called an acquaintance in the Governor's Office and set up a lunch meeting. The aide listened.

"It's something I can run by Governor Lingle. She says no, that's it. If, I'm only saying *if* she likes the idea, can she take complete credit for it?"

"No problem. She's the only one who can make it happen."

"And China would want credit, too." The woman twisted her mouth, thinking. "If they decide to go along, which is doubtful. Really, why should they? They'll say the jade is theirs. Give it back, no strings attached."

"We could use Amy's story at that point, but I don't think she'd like it publicized."

"We could use it without her name. How would that work? How many are we talking about? One? Two?"

"Amy suggested one woman for each of the four pieces."

"We'll be lucky to get two, probably one or none. The State Department has to pass on it. Immigration will have a fit. Homeland Security will jump all over us."

"That's why I came to you. Only the Governor can swing this one."

"How about infants or young children, orphans? Homeland Security can't say they're spies."

"Good thinking."

"Okay, Loxie, I'll see what I can do. Timing is critical. Give me a few days to broach this with the Governor."

"Sure."

*　　*　　*

After seven weeks, Governor Lingle announced a joint press conference with representatives of the US Diplomatic Corps, and the Chinese Government.

"Good morning, ladies and gentlemen. Today my colleagues and I are pleased to announce Project Jade, a joint undertaking by our two great countries to make a difference in the lives of four children. Four Chinese girls between the ages of seven and eleven years will receive training, through the university level, either in China or the US. When the time comes, and qualifications met, if these young women want to study in the US, I am pleased to announce the University of Hawaii will accept them, tuition-free. The United States of America and the State of Hawaii extend the hand of friendship across the Pacific to China.

"My colleague, Mr. Tsing Lai Shu, has more details for you." The Governor stepped back from the microphone and shook hands with China's representative.

"Today as a gesture of friendship between our great countries, I announce that China will pay the expense of educating four young women, orphans, through their advanced studies in Chinese cultural history. This gesture of appreciation we call Project Jade. We do this in gratitude for the return of four jade pieces stolen from the ancient tomb of Emperor Qin Shi Huang Di and in the recognition of a new era of friendship and cooperation between China and the United States. All the world recognizes the importance of Chinese cultural history. Project Jade is a new start for four children, and a new appreciation and recognition of the ancient treasures of China."

Loxie sent a video of the Honolulu newscast to Amy. The story received only a paragraph in the national news in California. A heightened alert for a possible terrorist threat, a forest fire in the Santa Cruz Mountains and other stories bumped their way into Bay Area headlines. Harv reached over and took Amy's hand in his while they watched the video of the Hawaii broadcast.

"You did it, Amy. You moved world powers to action. Those four little girls may never know the full extent of their good fortune."

"I wish them well," said Amy like a prayer. "It's a second chance. Some day I'd like to know they made it."

E-mail to Argus, Trez, three others
July: Harv and Amy's belated ten-day honeymoon

Harv and I went fishing this morning on *It's Time* with Captain Fran O'Brien. We had flat seas and a light breeze. Snow dusted the summit of Moana Kea. The white observatories shone in the sunshine. We ventured twelve or thirteen miles from the harbor, north to the Grounds and beyond. Haliakala on Maui snuggled in her Cumulus nest on the horizon. The early morning sun teased bluer blues from the sea and sky. Even the dry Kona coastline had a slight green cast from the recent rain. Harv said it was my imagination. Kohala, farther north, reflected more green.

We saw the smallest Humpback calf we have ever seen. Mama looked huge in comparison. Later, we saw the dorsal fins of two Tiger sharks. The sharks usually hunt alone and are all business. These two lolled on the surface, either courting or relaxed from a big breakfast.

We tagged and released a Blue Marlin. Captain Fran O'Brien estimated it to be 100-125 pounds. We picked up a nice thirty-six pound ono on the way back. We'll freeze part of it and bring it home in a cooler to share with you. Fran explained the airline requirements for transporting frozen fish. Jell packs, no ice and the cooler must be sealed with duct tape.

I have Sam Choy's recipe for mango-papaya salsa that's wonderful with fish.

Oh yes, Harv and I definitely plan to retire here.

Love, Amy

Epilogue

Thirty-three years later
Instant Message from Hale Moana O'Leigh
Kapaluu Beach, Kailua-Kona
To Trez, Mai, and eight others in California

Hi Everyone,

Harv and I went out fishing this morning under a dramatic sky. A thunderhead billowed and rained on the northern horizon. We saw small, isolated squalls to the southwest, nothing to cause alarm. We headed straight out from the harbor mouth about five miles, then turned south. I stopped paying attention and read the morning paper.

We picked up a small striped marlin, tagged and released it. I returned to the newspaper and didn't pay attention to the sea or sky until Harv said, "Whale!"

A Humpback surfaced close to us. The whale dove, and I paid more attention. I saw the wind line closing. The clouds moved from the top of Hualalai, Kailua-Kona's volcano, to the water and whitecaps

209

bounced angrily in the distance. The clouds moved in fast and low, like a soft, gray quilt. Other boats turned back toward the harbor. A few ran west, farther out to sea to try to outrun the wind and rain. I insisted we bring in the gear. The wind caught us before we had it all in. (Yes, Marilyn, this is where I would have told you to get your life jacket on and tie the top.)

Although I am sure the wind speed surprised Harv a little, he decided to run downwind to avoid the worst of it. You can imagine my reaction. This is not an isolated thunderhead with sunshine on either side. I objected. I didn't think we could outrun it.

We headed north into the face of the squall, but also the direction of the harbor, a good hour and a half away. Then, we turned south because it was so rough. Next, we tried west, farther out from shore. It all depended upon how much I whined and when. Rain and wind soaked through our canvas bimini top and drenched Harv and me. I hung on and stayed in my seat. At least my butt was dry. Not for long. I felt water running down my spine. So much sea spray came over the windshield I was reminded of *The Perfect Storm* (never a good film to watch before deep-sea fishing). The clouds closed us in. We could see one other boat but the land, the mountain, the Earth disappeared. Harv insisted he was still heading to the harbor. I wondered. We have a GPS, but neither of us had our glasses on. Salt water smudges the lenses and cannot be wiped away. I joked that at least the sea would feel warmer than the rain if we went into the water.

Holding tight and soaked to the skin, I considered the new details I wanted to add to my novel, but haven't yet. I thought about our grandchildren. I realized I have had a fabulous life. An exit now, when things like a knee here and there have begun to fall apart, wouldn't be so terrible.

Obviously, we made it back. The squall had washed through the harbor, continued south, caught us and kept going. The clean up on the boat was major. Everything not inside the cuddy cabin got wet except my purse, the logbook and your copy of *John Adams*, David. I'd put these items in a plastic bag.

On our way home, Harv tried to explain again why he wanted to go south. We had a lighthearted disagreement over the direction of the squall, inland or continued out to sea, or both. True, it was the first squall that caught us in all the times we've gone fishing.

I don't care. He owes me dinner.

Amy

About the Author

Linda Lanterman, one of the Sierra Writers, lives in Auburn, California and Kailua-Kona, Hawaii. Her rich sense of character and setting developed early. A Navy Junior, she attended schools in nine states and crisscrossed the rest. She fishes on *Lucky Linda* at Honokohau. *Transition in Green* is her fourth novel.